Dedicated to Caroline,
and to my sons,
Peter and Thomas

TALES OF GHOSTLY HORROR

Real-life Encounters with the Supernatural

BY

Peter Drake

Tales of Ghostly Horror:
Real-life Encounters with the Supernatural
©Peter Drake 2010
All rights reserved

ISBN: 978-1-4475-1932-4

Cover artwork and design by Suzanne Drake

CONTENTS

Introduction	7
1. The Haunted Farmhouse by the Fjord	11
2. Woodchester Mansion	17
3. The Thing in the Cellar: Haunting at a Herefordshire Farmhouse	27
4. The Galleries of Justice	36
5. Echoes of the Past: Haunting at Occupation Street, Dudley	54
6. The Station Hotel	61
7. Ouija Boards: Perilous Gateways into the Unknown	70
8. The Haunted Hospital	79
9. Haunting at Withymoor	90
10. The Albrighton Apparition	93
11. Haunting at Coseley	95
12. The Ancient Ram Inn	100
13. Conversation with a Murderer's Ghost	113
14. Haunting at Minehead	117
15. Caldicot Castle	119
16. The Pervy Poltergeist: Haunting at a Tanning Salon	122
17. Middleton Hall	125

18. The Hellfire Caves	129
19. Ghosts of Edinburgh	133
20. Theatre on the Steps	136
21. The Dixie Dude Ranch	139
22. The Haunted Church	143
23. World Oneiric Life Force: An overview	150

INTRODUCTION

"The oldest and strongest emotion of mankind is fear, and the oldest and strongest kind of fear is fear of the unknown."

— H.P. LOVECRAFT

I do not believe nor disbelieve anything on principle. To blindly accept or refute accounts of supernatural activity without considering the evidence would be irrational. It would be prejudiced. That is not the point of scepticism, which should encourage one to mistrust accepted beliefs and to maintain a healthy portion of doubt.

I am open to the possibility that the paranormal is real; yet sensible enough to realise that ghosts are not responsible for every 'bump in the night.' If asked, "Do I believe in ghosts?" I would have to say, "I don't know."

The stories in this collection originate from interviews with people who honestly maintain that they have encountered supernatural entities and disturbances. I have faith that they showed integrity when discussing their experiences with me. It can be difficult to avoid reacting with incredulity when faced with reports of poltergeists and apparitions, for there is reluctance to believe in things that you cannot or did not see. This is particularly true with ghosts. I have tried to avoid judgements; I have simply attempted to tell people's stories and to impart their fear of the unknown.

H.P. Lovecraft (1890-1937) was a groundbreaking writer of supernatural fiction. He believed that 'cosmic fear' was the only genuine form of horror:

> *"The one test of the really weird is simply this – whether or not there be excited in the reader a profound sense of dread, and of contact with unknown spheres and powers; a subtle attitude of awed listening, as if for the beating of black wings or the scratching of outside shapes and entities on the known universe's utmost rim."*

This was his definition of fear. Readers of this tome might get that same hint of nameless, shapeless forces outside of our comprehension - of things that exist in the darker corners of existence, scratching at our mundane world.

The difference is that these are *real-life* stories. They are not fictional.

I have collaborated with 'World Oneiric Life Force' – or WOLF, for short. WOLF is a team based in the West Midlands, England, which specialises in paranormal research and spiritual healing. It was founded in 2006 by Simone Taylor and David Ball. In recent years, they have recruited to the WOLF team, adding to its incredibly diverse range of talents.

The current roster is:

- Simone Taylor (Clairsentient/Developing Trance Medium)
- David Ball (Clairvoyant/Angel Cards Psychic Profiler)
- Liz Cormell (Spiritual Consultant, Claircognient)
- Paul Dyason (Data Analyst)
- Rachel Penny (Research Assistant, Data Logger)
- Vanessa Penny (Historical Researcher)
- Gemma Taylor (Events leader, Spirit-sensitive)

There are several associate members involved in investigations, including:

- Julie Bennett
- Kevin Berrill
- Dawn Goding

This book is the combination of interviews with WOLF members of staff; my own experiences at paranormal investigations; and interviews with ordinary members of the public, who did not wish to be named and have been given a pseudonym to avoid identification.

All errors are mine.

The real experts are WOLF, and they can be found at their website - **www.wolf-rs.co.uk**. There is an active chat forum for discussion, and public investigations are held regularly.

Acknowledgement is given to the assistance of Vanessa Penny, Rachel Penny, Simone Taylor, Liz Cormell, Dawn Goding and Paul Dyason – many thanks for your time and conversation.

Special acknowledgement is given to Suzanne Drake, whose cover artwork makes me feel ever so proud.

* Note to readers in the U.S.A. and rest of the world: all locations discussed in this book are in Great Britain, with the exception of Dixie Dude Ranch in Texas, U.S.A, and a farmhouse in Norway.

The Haunted Farmhouse by the Fjord

Interview with Jemma (pseudonym)

Jemma is a perfectly ordinary young woman: she works as a health care professional in the West Midlands, living with her boyfriend and their dog, and struggling to cope with a mortgage. She seemed more worried about nearing the age of thirty than anything else.

An unexpected financial windfall gave them the opportunity for an overseas holiday, and they set their hearts on Scandinavia. They loved the idea of roaming the countryside and getting away from crowds, and the thought of long, summer nights was romantic. She never imagined that her holiday would have her trapped in a haunted farmhouse and desperate to escape.

Because of its northerly latitude, the summers in Norway have long hours of daylight, and around the time of the midsummer solstice the evenings never really darken for long. In contrast, the winters have extremely long nights where the sun rises for just a few hours.

Jemma and her boyfriend hired a large, traditional farmhouse in the Norwegian fjords, where the sea runs for many miles inland along rivulets and through narrow passes in the mountainous landscape. After arriving at the location the couple were surprised by how remarkably eerie it appeared to be. Reality upset their expectations. "The countryside was bleak," said Jemma, "it wasn't so populated as the countryside in our country. It was different. There were whole swathes where no one went to."

She was also surprised by the area around their holiday accommodation. The farmhouse was just a few metres from the sea and surrounded by orchards, on the outskirts of a small settlement. It was far from civilisation, and this perturbed Jemma: "We had the hills and mountains on one side, and on the other side there was the sea, so I felt boxed in and trapped. It was creepy because of the water - I'm scared of water — and it was quiet, you couldn't hear any birds, there were no animal or traffic noises, not even the sound of the sea. It was disturbingly quiet.

"The daylight was weird, not what I'm used to. Most of it was like twilight, not very bright. I kept expecting it to get dark but it never did. I think it would have been worse in winter with permanent darkness."

The farmhouse was not what they had anticipated, even after taking into account that it was in a foreign country with a different sense of décor to Britain's. It was outdated, almost unchanged from the 1960s, and the dark wooden panelling gave an impression of deep shadows. Photographs of dying deer shot by hunters were morbidly hung in many of the rooms. There was a horribly twisting staircase to the upper floor, and doors to several rooms were locked. This did nothing to appease their paranoia over the coming week.

The atmosphere was heavy and thick, pressing in upon them.

"It seemed like someone had died in there," said Jemma. "It was like the kind of house you'd get locked up in and tortured, or see a terrified face at a window when driving past. I kept thinking of witches, maybe because of a big, old-fashioned picture at the top of the stairs, showing a house in a forest. I kept thinking that this was the house in the picture, and that it was a haunted house."

Even the landlord behaved peculiarly when she showed the couple around the property. What struck Jemma was the odd way the landlord reacted, almost flinching, when they said which bedroom they would be using.

This was the main bedroom of the house, and Jemma hated it:

> *"I really didn't like the main bedroom. I didn't like the cupboards which lined the entire wall on the one side of the room. It was hollow behind them, and it was like a long corridor where you could walk if you stooped.*
>
> *"I always had the feeling of being watched in that room. It wasn't so bad in the daytime, but I still felt it, and I was glad to get downstairs. It was much worse at night. I didn't even like getting undressed.*

> *"I didn't like the first night, it was creepy in that room. When I was in bed I didn't want to turn away from my boyfriend, I snuggled up to him, in case I saw something standing there looking at me. I didn't want to say anything to him because I didn't want to seem like a scaredy-cat. The next day he told me that he had saw something, some kind of a ghost."*

During the night Jemma's boyfriend had woken slightly, opening his eyes. At the bottom of the bed he had seen standing there a "shadowy figure," which was looking at them as they slept and was now staring directly at him. It knew that he was awake. Jemma's boyfriend had admitted to her that he had been scared, and had felt an urge to cover his face, or shut his eyes and pretend that he was asleep so that nothing would happen to him. He did not want to be noticed by the thing in the room.

In hindsight he acknowledged that it could have just been a 'waking dream' accentuated by unusual shadows in a strange room. He had felt uneasy in the house after they had arrived, the same as Jemma, but had not told her until the next morning in order to avoid worrying her.

"At first I thought he was joking, trying to scare me," she said. "I was not very pleased. It confirmed my fears, and was disconcerting. I felt even worse after that! I didn't feel altogether safe afterwards. It was a little better when we put some suitcases up against the door [at night] but as the door opened outwards it wasn't much of an obstacle."

They were never comfortable after that, and Jemma seems to have had growing feelings of dread.

"The house felt malicious or malignant," she said, "as if something was in there and it didn't like us. I know that all houses have a different feel – some are nice and others feel bad. This one had a really bad atmosphere. It felt like something was following us, watching us, and I never felt entirely secure. There were weird noises at night, in the other bedrooms and the bathroom. My boyfriend went to check, but he didn't like to!"

They saw the landlord on a few more occasions, and she was peculiarly worried that they thought something was wrong with the house. Her questions seemed unnecessary, and prompted by something other than friendly concern. Jemma connected this interest with their experiences in the farmhouse. She feels that the landlord knew that the house was haunted.

The week passed quickly for the couple as they enjoyed travelling and sightseeing in the region. They took trips into the mountains, hiking through wild valleys and joining boat trips along the fjords. They liked Norway.

Every evening at the farmhouse their unease would return. It increased as the hours passed. Though it never became truly dark outside with the midsummer twilight, the house seemed filled with perpetual gloom.

"I didn't want to go upstairs for the rest of the week," Jemma declared, "and I would not have slept in the house by myself. I hated it when my boyfriend went outside to look at the sea and drink a cup of tea. I couldn't stand being by myself in the house and I had to make excuses for going out to him.

"It got worse, a growing sense that something wasn't right. It was building like electricity. I was glad to leave before anything else happened."

Woodchester Mansion

Personal account of a WOLF paranormal investigation

The woodland was thickening as we went deeper into the valley. It was getting dark, and we had driven for what seemed like ages across that long, broken path. At last we passed a tight corner to see our destination for the night, Woodchester Mansion. Even at this far distance it loomed ominously: an old Victorian hall, abandoned in such a lonely spot. Where better for an all-night ghost-hunt?

I was invited to a paranormal investigation at Woodchester Mansion, organised by WOLF. It was a large gathering of people, as the event was open to members of the public: nineteen guests were participating in the night's activities. Five WOLF staff members were there to share their keen psychic sensitivity, including Simone Taylor, David Ball, Vanessa Penny, Rachel Penny and Gemma Taylor.

I topped up the number of people to twenty-five, attending the event as a neutral observer. Like many of the guests, I am open-minded in my opinions on the supernatural - I neither believe nor disbelieve – and it was interesting for a 'newbie' such as me to visit Woodchester.

Woodchester's notoriety

I was vaguely familiar with Woodchester Mansion's reputation for paranormal activity. It has featured on TV shows such as 'Scariest Places on Earth' and 'Scream Team.' Sinister sightings have included headless horsemen and Roman soldiers; there are reports of wandering spirits, apparitions and weird smells. When 'Most Haunted' held a vigil at the location in 2005, they captured activity such as strange noises and moving tables.

The building itself is a bizarre relic of Victorian gothic architecture. It is located in a secluded Cotswold valley, in Gloucestershire, and it is definitely 'out-of-the-way', and not easy to reach. It is in the hollow of a valley, where woodland on every side encircles the mansion clearing. "It looked very scary indeed," said WOLF's Gemma Taylor. "It was in such a deserted location."

At night, there is absolute silence.

The mansion appears to be a complete building only from the outside. A grand renovation was mysteriously abandoned in 1868 when workers dropped their tools and left, never to return. No refurbishment has subsequently taken place, and there are whole sections of the internal building missing. In many places there are no proper ceilings or floors, no plasterwork or doors and furnishings. There is only the monumental stone infrastructure. The architecture is beautiful: there are decorated columns, and ornate, vaulted ceilings, with spiral staircases and labyrinthine corridors. I saw large empty rooms without plaster and without floors, and looking over balconies, I could see vast open drops that were murky black with their depths.

Séance in the chapel

The investigation began with a séance in the chapel. All the guests gathered in a circle, and, as space was limited, I remained in the archway along with Gemma, Rachel and Vanessa.

The lights were turned off, plunging everything into blackness. For a few minutes the atmosphere was calm and still, with Simone and David challenging spirits to show themselves. As I grew accustomed to the dark I saw tiny glints of light shining through the windows from outside. It did not really matter, as I still could barely see a thing.

Simone became aware of a male energy entering the room.

"He did not seem particularly interested in any one person," she said afterwards. "He seemed to only want to observe. I was giving my full attention, trying to get information as to who he was. I was startled at a stronger energy coming up to me from the right side and I felt and saw a very dark shadow push up towards my face. I stepped back slightly in surprise and it quickly moved away. During this time the name John was given to me intuitively."

David seemed to sense a different male energy: older, stronger, and with an unusual physical appearance, his face being ugly and mangled. "This energy was not frightening but slightly imposing," he said. "I could see him in my mind's eye walking around the circle, leering into people's faces, including mine!"

Some of us who were standing near the archway heard a male groan from somewhere in the adjoining part of the chapel. This section contained scaffolding and had a high ceiling, with evidence of plans for a huge stained-glass window. The groan happened not long after the séance began, and I heard it distinctly.

People saw shadows in the séance circle. Participants also experienced strange sensations, such as gentle touching, a breeze rushing past them, and light anomalies. Flashes of red light were explained by peoples' cameras, and small white flashes were caused by minute reflections from spectacles. But for several reports of a purple light anomaly in the centre of the circle, there were no explanations.

I could swear that I saw this purplish flash myself. I was looking into the chapel where the séance was taking place, which was completely dark. I happened to see a quick flash of light in the middle of the room. It was bright, purplish, and moving like a gash in the air. It was momentary, and as it disappeared I perceived some kind of deepening shadow in front of that same spot which then itself evaporated. I had no idea what it was, and did not see it again. I did not mention it to anyone until I had heard that other people had seen the same thing.

The séance also helped David and Simone to become aware of a child, perhaps a little girl's spirit, and Simone was intuitively given the letter J, followed by a name which could have been Jean or Jeanette. The child moved around the circle, and guests commented on a cold feeling around their legs.

Not long after this the atmosphere grew quiet again, and it was decided that we would split into smaller groups to hold vigils in different locations throughout the building.

A dark energy in the cellar

The cellar is an epicentre of activity at Woodchester Mansion. On previous investigations the WOLF team discovered a dark energy that dwelt there. Tensions were high as the team entered the cellar on their initial scout of the location before the guests arrived.

A door opened to the cellar, which was accessed by steep stairs. As I descended, I saw that the ceiling was vaulted and ridged, narrowing towards the bottom almost like a throat. Below lay the place where the WOLF team had seen a shadowy, amorphous thing which had been 'aware' of them. "The only way I can describe this entity is as a negative soul that never rests," David said later, "and I seem to see it in the form of black smoke." He later compared it to the black, smoke-like entity in the TV programme 'Lost.'

People felt uncomfortable in the cellar. "As we descended the staircase, a sense of uneasiness drew upon myself," said David. Fresh batteries in cameras died immediately, and Rachel saw a heavy wooden door start to swing open by itself. As we climbed the stairs to leave the cellar, some heard a faint shuffling sound coming from behind us.

There were several vigils in the cellar after the chapel séance. The twenty five people divided into smaller groups. During his group's vigil in the cellar, David psychically sensed the presence of a pack of dogs being fed meat by "a tall, butch fellow with a bloody white apron...like Leatherface from 'Texas Chainsaw Massacre.'"

"After calling out to him he did seem to then engage with us and once he saw us he became a little unnerved himself. This is something I have never seen before."

During a glass divination session in the cellar, there seemed to be a spirit trying to impersonate a guest's family member, and David was led to believe that they were communicating with the negative entity in the cellar.

Rachel also tried glass divination in one of the cellar's rooms, and it developed that her group was in contact with a male spirit that had killed people in the mansion, and now wished to harm one of the investigators in the house. Understandably there were a few people upset by this news.

Many vigils in the old mansion house

My smaller group headed to the third floor at the top of the house, where paranormal activity had been reported on previous investigations. There was a long corridor, with almost no light, and we stood at the farthest end, away from the staircase.

We conducted a séance. At the opposite end there was a luminous sign; it was bright but difficult to focus on due to the distance. Some people were adamant that a dark form was moving in front of the sign, blurring it. I was sceptical, as it seemed blurred to me because my eyes were straining to see in the dark. Tests to judge the phenomenon were inconclusive, and I did not sense anything unduly strange.

We moved and held a vigil in the bathroom. This was a peculiar place, with a large, stone bath. Simone helped a guest to use a dowsing pendulum for divining.[1] I observed the group as they spoke to the male energy Simone encountered in the chapel, and they discovered that the little girl Simone had sensed earlier was his daughter.

---

[1] Pendulum dowsing is an attempt to gain information from spirits by gauging the swaying (or lack of swaying) of the pendulum in response to questions, perhaps spelling out words or making simple 'yes/no' answers.

Other groups that held vigils in the bathroom experienced stones being thrown during séances, and I observed that a trigger object that had been moved.

There were a range of experiences. One guest saw an old lady walking down a corridor towards her. Vanessa heard heavy and repeated banging, and felt a sharp drop in temperature as she managed a vigil on the 2nd floor.

"His face was transforming…I was terrified!"

Several groups met on the third floor, including mine. This was where there had been consternation at the luminous sign. A man now claimed that he had sudden difficulties breathing, and that he had never felt like this before. Then it was Gemma's turn to feel terror.

Earlier during the chapel séance, Gemma had sensed a male spirit in the chapel whose name was Tom. As she now looked at Paul Dyason (now a WOLF staff member, but at this time a member of the public), he seemed to transform before her eyes into the semblance of Tom.

"This spirit was staring at me, trying to tell me something," Gemma said. "He seemed very powerful, very strong."

She was frightened and moved away from Paul. Another guest shared her disquiet, agreeing that she could see Paul's face morphing. I could feel everyone's nerves become highly-strung. To my eyes, in that darkened place, Paul had not changed and his face was unaltered.

"Ghosts were frightened by seeing 'real' people!"

The night was very cold, and by dawn the stone floors helped to make my feet feel like blocks of ice. Time had passed very quickly. The event closed down, and we went home.

This was my first experience of a paranormal investigation, and I confirmed to myself that I am not overly-sensitive to the supernatural. I understand that close encounters with the supernatural are rare, but that 'quiet' places can unexpectedly blaze into paranormal activity. From the outside, Woodchester appears to be a very strange, gothic mansion. Internally, with the archaic architecture and vast, open spaces it is a feast for the imagination. However, I did not feel anything too unsettling. On this occasion, I was not convinced that the building had a bad atmosphere. There were one or two moments that I could not explain, but on this night it was not buzzing with paranormal activity.

What could explain many of the sights and sounds I had experienced? Was it eyestrain from looking too hard in the dark? Were echoes and footfalls magnified into something creepy in that empty shell of a house?

David Ball has suggested that many reported incidents could be the result of 'residual' energy from the many previous buildings that have stood on the site since the 16th century. It is important to remember that the existing Woodchester Mansion has never been extensively lived in, and only certain rooms have ever been inhabited for any length of time. Perhaps the things that are seen at Woodchester are psychic echoes from previous buildings.

David's encounter with Leatherface in the cellar was significant. One theory suggests that ghosts and spirits are perhaps entities on another plane of existence, perhaps people in the past seen through some kind of window in time and space. Maybe Leatherface saw David and thought, "Bloody hell, it's a demon!" The idea that ghosts were frightened by seeing us 'real' people is amusing.

The Thing in the Cellar:
Haunting at a Herefordshire Farmhouse

Interviews with Liz Cormell,

Rachel Penny and Vanessa Penny

As young children, Vanessa Penny and her sister Rachel spent time at their uncle's farmhouse in Peterchurch. This is a village along the River Dore, not far from Hereford in an area known as 'The Golden Valley.'

The farmhouse was in a lonely place. It was approached along a narrow lane, with few houses nearby. Originally there was a monastery on the site, which had been demolished and replaced with houses. Their uncle's farmhouse retained features of the religious building, such as a cellar and many gravestones running along the frontage.

No wonder that the sisters thought the place was "spooky."

There were a number of small, unusual things that caught their attention. Lights would turn on and off by themselves. Pens would go missing and suddenly turn up in an obvious place. Then there was the cellar.

The cellar seemed to be the focus of all the strange activity. Vanessa sometimes heard footsteps in there and upon the cellar steps, even though there was no one down there and the door was shut. Their uncle meticulously bolted the cellar door every night; but in the morning he sometimes found the door unlocked and wide open. They had no idea how this happened, or who could have done it. Nothing else had been disturbed. "It was like mischievous children were playing games with us," said Vanessa.

Her sister, Rachel, had a much more terrifying experience with the thing in the cellar:

> *"When I was a kid, around eleven or twelve years old, I used to be locked in the cellar by my aunt as a punishment. I don't think my uncle ever knew about it. When I was naughty, she used to get me and put me in there and lock the door. She'd leave me in there for a few minutes.*
>
> *"It was pitch black in the cellar, the only light was at the bottom of the door coming through from the house. The cellar door was at the top of stairs, and I used to sit and wait at the top of these stairs.*
>
> *"The staircase went down to a graveyard. There were gravestones at the bottom of the cellar, and probably people were still buried down there.*
>
> *"This one time she put me in there, it took a while for my eyes to adjust to the dark. I was sitting at the top of the*

stairs. As my eyes adjusted, I could see a figure at the bottom.

"It was in a black robe, some kind of old-fashioned vicar, with the black long coats they used to wear, with black trousers but not a white collar.

"It was staring straight at me.

"I started screaming. I was screaming for ten minutes before my aunt let me out.

"It was the first spirit I encountered. It stayed with me, this spirit. I could sense it with my third eye [psychically] *and it forced me to block myself off at first. It followed me about for a long time, and I could sense it everywhere – at work, while shopping at Merry Hill, in the 'Singing Caverns' at the Black Country Museum.*

"I don't think the spirit was evil. There was nothing evil there at the house, it was just curious and wondered what I was up to."

In the past, the old monastery was connected to a chapel at the bottom of the lane by a tunnel running from the monastery's cellar, which was used by monks for getting to the chapel without being seen. It is perhaps not surprising that the cellar was a focus of paranormal incidents, with its history as a thoroughfare and the gravestones left behind. Perhaps there were still corpses in the graves, too.

Supernatural hotspot of Herefordshire

Peterchurch seems to attract paranormal incidents and coincidences. It is only a small village, yet there seem to be a proportionally high number of disturbances. People living at a four hundred year-old house in the village reported that their kitchen bin was thrown over repeatedly when they were not in the room. The apparition of an old woman in 1800s period clothing was also seen looking out from an attic window at the house.[2]

The property next door to the Penny's farmhouse has had trouble with the supernatural. This suggests that it might be something that affects the entire location, not limited to one particular house or set of people. There was alleged poltergeist activity at the neighbour's house when a connecting door between this property and the next one along was blocked. "They kept hearing a knocking on this boarded-up door and it went on for months," said Vanessa. This was the ghost of an old woman, who used to pass through the door regularly before she died. When the barrier was removed, the knocking stopped.

---

[2] http://www.pebblesspiritualcave.com/Shaun.html

Peterchurch and the surrounding area have an unusual historical tradition. Research has unearthed some startling coincidences that suggest that the Penny's tales of ghostly horrors may not be without merit.

The concept of ley lines was first proposed by Alfred Watkins in the early 1920s after he travelled around this part of Herefordshire.[3] He noticed that there were footpaths connecting many of the hilltops in a straight line. More significantly, he saw that local landmarks such as Arthur's Stone, Urishay Castle, Snodhill Castle and Longtown Castle, ran in a straight line southwards towards the Skirrid Fawr Mountain in Monmouthshire, Wales. This is the same mountain where stands 'The Skirrid Inn,' reputed to be one of the most haunted places in the British Isles.

Mr. Watkins's theory had nothing to do with the supernatural: he thought ley lines had an archaeological importance, showing ancient pathways that were possibly pre-Roman or Neolithic in origin, used for trade or ceremonial purposes. This would be true of the Golden Valley, in which nestles Peterchurch: there is evidence that it was inhabited in ancient times, from late Palaeolithic into the Mesolithic and Neolithic periods.

---

[3] http://www.absoluteastronomy.com/topics/Ley_line

The Peterchurch well and its myths

It also has a place in the legendary, possibly far-fetched travels of St. Peter and St. Paul around Britain. On their way to Wales they stopped at the Golden Valley, where St. Peter is supposed to have blessed a well at a nearby natural spring – probably St. Peter's Well – and here he baptised converts to Christianity. The settlement that grew around the church later became (unsurprisingly) Peterchurch.

Even the name for the 'Golden Valley' has a mythical origin, receiving its name from a trout that was caught in the river with a golden chain around its neck, with some versions of the story saying that it was St. Peter himself that caught the fish and placed a golden chain on it, keeping it in the nearby Holy Well. This well – St. Peter's Well, in Peterchurch – was historically reputed to have healing powers, and used extensively for the cure of rheumatism and sore eyes.

The presence of holy wells in the Golden Valley caused trouble in the later Middle Ages, when church authorities took severe offence at the pagan-like worship of a stone and well in Turnastone, a parish just south of Peterchurch. In 1409 the Bishop of Hereford is supposed to have issued a proclamation condemning the congregations in his diocese for making offerings and prayers at the well and stone; this was idolatrous, a risk to their eternal souls. Under threat of excommunication, people were banned from worshipping at the stone and well, and from even visiting them.

Ancient entities from the astral plane

Gary Varner, a writer interested in the myths of Holy Wells, describes how the fish at St. Peter's Well was thought to have supernatural characteristics.[4] It was a guardian of sorts for Pagan worshippers, possessing eternal life and wisdom, existing as a link to the gods and the Otherworld. This sounds like the modern idea of an elemental.

'Elementals' have been described as creatures of conscious energy. They are invisible entities from other dimensions and planes of existence, called into our world through incantations, Ouija boards and other portals. They have been given myriad epithets throughout history - some people call them demons, others have called them dryads, nymphs, spirits of the forests, fairies, goblins – and they are thought to be older than the human race.

"In times past when people were in tune with natural energies, they might ask for help or protection, calling upon elementals in trees and rivers," explained Liz Cormell. "Once raised the energies would stay unless the portal they came through was closed. Some of them are ancient. These energies or elementals have intelligence.

---

[4] See Gary R. Varner, *Sacred Wells: A Study in the History, Meaning, and Mythology of Holy Wells and Waters,* 2009

They are not evil, and they are not like the devil. Elementals have purposes that can be at odds with what we want, so they oppose us and we call them 'evil.'"

Some experts hold elementals responsible for much of the reported poltergeist-type activity, such as tapping and banging, objects being moved or thrown, drafts and cold spots.[5] They can escape if called into our world and not properly contained or sent back, remaining here as tricksters, feeding off people's energies. They are infinitely malleable, and can change their appearance to suit the mental imagery and expectations of the people that catch glimpses of them.

It gives pause for thought that the phenomenon at Peterchurch could be attributed to the presence of these entities. This does not discount the involvement of spirits, the souls of deceased people that roam our world. It is all a matter of opinion as to the causes of paranormal activity – there may not be a single reason or cause.

This historical background offers a surprising level of coincidence. Vanessa and Rachel were unaware that Peterchurch and its environs were so replete with historical, paranormal and spiritual significance.

---

[5] See J. Edward Cornelious, *Aleister Crowley and the Ouija Board*, 2005

"Cats don't play tunes!"

The Penny's were not lucky with their Herefordshire ghosts. They lived in a house in Hereford and this too was haunted. "We had a ghost that played the piano and scared our baby sitter to death," said Vanessa. "Mum and Dad went out one evening and warned her that the cat sometimes went up and down the piano keys. When they got back, the baby sitter had barricaded herself in the living room.

"When Mum asked her why she had done that, she said, 'Cats don't play tunes!'"

The Galleries of Justice[6]

Interviews with Liz Cormell, Dawn Goding, Rachel Penny, Vanessa Penny and Simone Taylor

A long and bloody history hangs over the Galleries of Justice. It was once the beating heart of law and order in Nottingham, incorporating a gaol, courthouse and gallows; and it claims with brutal honesty to have been "the only site where you could be arrested, sentenced and executed in one building."[7] Now it is preserved as a Grade II listed museum, showcasing the horrors of its past.

It is considered one of the most haunted places in Britain. Television programmes such as 'Most Haunted' have enhanced its reputation for unexplained activity, and the location has become notorious for supernatural phenomenon. There have been sightings of ghosts, such as spectral soldiers seen walking through walls; footsteps have been heard in cell corridors, and disembodied voices and sudden bangs have terrified people; many light anomalies have been photographed.

The Galleries of Justice are in the Lace Market area of Nottingham, which was part of Nottingham's original Saxon settlement and later a focus point for Norman

---

[6] Many thanks to Vanessa Penny and her historical research on the Galleries of Justice

[7] As stated by Tim Desmond, Chief Executive of Galleries of Justice

jurisdiction in the county. It first appeared in written records in 1375, when it was used as a court, and later as a prison in 1449. Executions and corporal punishment such as whippings and beatings were carried out here for many centuries. Its role as a centre of justice was only curtailed in modern times, as the police station was in operation until 1986 and the courts shut in 1985. Among its relics are a large collection of artefacts related to crime and punishment, a pair of Victorian courthouses, a prison, a police station, and 'The Pits,' a series of cells within a medieval cave system that were used primarily for the confinement and punishment of prisoners.

The apparition in the chapel

There are four levels to the pyramid-like Galleries: the courtroom level at the top, descending to judge level, then prison level and finally to the cells in the caves. WOLF staff members seem convinced that the caves are the most paranormally active area in the Galleries of Justice, and their most active section is reputedly the chapel; it is not an official chapel as such, though some believe it was used for religious purposes previously. The caves go deep into the earth. This is the darkest, gloomiest part of the Galleries of Justice.

Simone Taylor and Gemma Woolridge (formerly a WOLF staff member) visited the Galleries in 2007 on a reconnaissance trip prior to a public investigation. They interviewed staff for a few 'real' ghost stories to share with the public, briefly looking around the location and never expecting to find anything.

Simone was utterly gobsmacked by what turned up:

> *"The chapel with a cave leading off now has a door at the entrance with bars at face level, where prisoners would have been able to look out. We were looking through these bars and asking out, with respect, for spirits to make themselves known – as you do. Firstly something was thrown from the cave area across the chapel floor. It was possibly a rock or stone, but as there was hay or straw on the floor it was difficult to determine the cause for sure.*
>
> *"That was exciting in itself, but after a minute or so of standing there we saw a misty black haze start to form in the cave entrance. We both had a rush of excitement; perhaps it was fear, yet strangely we had a very calming feeling flow through us as we slowly started to realise something was trying to manifest itself. After focusing for what seemed like ages I could make out the faint outline of a figure standing in the archway. We stood watching for over*

a minute before it gradually started to fade away, and we could no longer see any outline or surrounding mist in the area.

"That in itself was amazing, but it got better. We were both excited at having such an amazing experience. We thought that out of respect we would leave the area, and thanked the spirit for working so hard to show itself to us. As we walked away Gemma turned around and shouted, "Oh my God, look!"

"We both saw a face looking through the bars at us! The face was like a fuzzy, slightly shaded black colour, with a fairly clear outline. We could both make out the eyes which were staring straight at us. We grabbed each other's hands as a rush of adrenaline shot through us both at this spirit standing no less than five feet away and watching us. We slowly moved forwards towards it and I was overwhelmed with a feeling of sadness and unmistakeable feeling of it having being wrongly accused. It was almost like this spirit was asking for help.

"The image that appeared was extremely transparent so we could just about make out the outline of a long shaped face with very hollow looking eyes. The head was perfectly round so I can only assume the apparition had no hair. The eyes seemed very sunk back with deep hollow sockets, again very transparent, so faint but strangely clear. If I try and compare it to other 'real' images I have seen it would be most closely described to Lord of the Rings' Gollum but definitely not with a devious or evil look, it was a very sad and longing face – almost like it was reaching out in desperation and pain. We only saw the face as the gap in the bars was at head height. On reflection it would be difficult to know if it was male or female as I suspect that anyone thrown down the caves would be in that bad a state you would not be able to tell, although the lack of hair and the 'feeling' we got would suggest it was most probably male.

"We could clearly see the spirit for almost two minutes before it gradually faded away. During the

> *whole process we attempted communication, asking gentle questions, seeing if he needed help. We said we would be back in a few weeks and would love to see him again. Walking away from the chapel door was really difficult for me and Gemma. We had encountered full spirit contact and both witnessed exactly the same thing. This surely goes down as one of my top three ghostly experiences, one which will stay with me forever more."*

WOLF investigates the Galleries

WOLF has held several public investigations at the Galleries, and they have proved hugely memorable for the paranormal activity they encountered. People have been shocked and horrified by what they have discovered.

"My first visit to the Galleries of Justice was fantastic," said Liz Cormell. "There's a heavy atmosphere and it feels like a church. It's very oppressive. I spent time with a friend who was sceptical but interested. We were standing in the back gallery of the courtroom and I felt something behind me. It went really cold, and both of us felt that there was a cold spot on the rail. I thought, "Oh my God, weird!" I got emotional – it felt like I was watching a trial, like I was watching a loved one being tried but that there was no hope, that the decision was predetermined."

The courtrooms are hubs for weirdness. Mysterious dark figures are seen on the courtroom balcony, where many orbs have been captured on film.[8] Liz attributes this phenomenon to the strong emotions that have surged through the courtroom, leaving behind 'residual energy.' "[This] is a sort of replay," she said. "It can be in the fabric of a building or an object. Like sitting in a chair all the time, it leaves energy in an object. A lot of emotion has happened at the Galleries, and it's got to have an effect, the energy left by really emotional events like people being sentenced in court or tortured in the caves."

Among the consequences of this residual energy could be apparitions, if they are truly "echoes of past events." Heavy prison or death sentences were doled out in the courtrooms; on occasion, bodies of executed prisoners were brought in for dissection. These traumatic episodes could have imprinted on the spiritual fabric and affected the courtroom's energies in a way that resonates into future time and space.

Dawn Goding had an uneasy turn on her first visit to the courtroom:

> *"I was standing away from everyone else, by a clock at the back. The*

---

[8] Orbs are light anomalies that can be picked up on photographs or film footage. They are said to indicate spiritual activity.

> *medium who was with us looked up at me and said that someone was with me. My sister looked and she said there were two shadows by me – I looked and I could see another shadow behind me. They both couldn't have been my shadow, as there was only one light shining in this part of the courtroom. The medium said the shadow was that of a woman in green petticoats, a ghost who had been the wife of someone tried in the court."*

While Dawn had been standing by the clock she had images in her mind's eye of a courtroom in full working operation, and it felt like she was watching things happen, like a sort of replay.[9] "I can get something like photos come into my head," she said. "You question yourself – are you cold reading a place? Sometimes these things can pop up from your sub-conscious, but other times you can never have heard of them. It's very rare if you can come up with names and stuff not in documents."

Unexplained incidents have dogged other parts of the Galleries. WOLF was conducting a séance in the women's quarters, and everyone was holding hands:

---

[9] The 'mind's eye or 'third eye' is a higher state of consciousness which allows mental abilities such as clairvoyance, visions, and awareness of spirits. It is a concept common to many religions and cultures.

"One lady started getting very anxious," Simone Taylor said. "She told us that something was gripping her arm very tight and was hurting her. At this time everyone was linking hands so nobody could have influenced this event. I left the circle to investigate and I saw she had got a clear hand print on her arm where you could make out three fingers that had been holding on very tightly."

This happened at the same location on a different occasion, when another lady expressed discomfort at pain in her arm. She became so distressed that she had to leave the room.

Pitched into darkness

After a recent WOLF public investigation at the Galleries of Justice ended, everyone left the buildings until only Simone, David Ball and Paul Dyason remained. They were sitting in a corridor that leads to the chapel. Without warning, stones were thrown at them, hitting them on the back and arms. The WOLF staff did not know where the stones had come from, whether they had fallen from the ceiling or had been thrown. They felt that it was more likely the stones were thrown, as they had hit them horizontally. There was no one else in the area. Specially-set up cameras indicated that no one else had entered.

There have been many reports of stones thrown in this corridor. Not everybody is entirely convinced that it has a paranormal explanation. Liz Cormell has been hit with stones at this spot, but refers to a light shaft above the corridor that goes up to street level, speculating that the stones could have fallen from above, bouncing in different directions as they fell. Dawn Goding is also sceptical about the throwing of stones: "The caves in Nottingham are all made of sandstone, which falls apart when it's wet. After I've been in the caves at the Galleries I have little bits of sandstone in my hair afterwards, and I have to wash my hair a few times to get it all out. When people think they have stones hit them it might just be bits of sandstone falling off the walls and ceilings by themselves."

The venture into the caves took a turn for the worse for Simone, David and Paul. The light in everyone's torch inexplicably went off at the same time, casting the area into pitch-black darkness. "It was absolutely terrifying," said Simone, "My adrenaline was really going!"

Something was in the cave with them. Though Simone could not see anything in the gloomy dark, she could sense it. "I could feel something down there," she said, "I could feel the energy. I could hear a thrumming down there, like the air was vibrating. Dave said he could see whatever it was and he said that it looked like the terror-dogs from 'Ghostbusters.'"

"Something in the darkness was watching us"

Liz Cormell had the most frightening experience of her life in the chapel:

"The scariest thing I have ever had happen to me was in the caves. I was with Dave, Paul and Julie, along with members of the public, standing together in the middle of the chapel; it's a big circular room with a column in the centre. We were being circle. Something in the darkness was watching us and moving around the group. Things were coming up, looking at us and then backing off. The atmosphere was changing constantly, it got darker then lighter and then darker again. It was oppressive.

"Some members of the public were dubious about what we were saying, to say the least; but a couple who were with us and sensitive to spiritual energies said, "They're around us." Something was going on but we couldn't reason what it was.

"Basically I just shut down, I felt like I was going to panic. The feeling I had was like when someone makes you jump and your heart races. I was getting the physical sensation of things rushing towards me and stopping just short, really trying to

get my attention. But I didn't want to listen at all. It was more than tiredness or fear of caves or claustrophobia. I felt like I was going to be tortured. It was a psychic attack, really negative and very powerful. Normally I can tell if something is messing about, and I'm confident about my power - I'm in control, I can protect myself. But this time I knew if I let them [the entities] near me, I'd go to pieces. It felt more powerful than I could cope with.

"I tried to think of white light, I forced myself to stay in control. Nobody said anything to me about it; I don't think they noticed until afterwards when I was quieter than usual. But the woman who had been sitting next to me in the chapel knew something was wrong as I had been holding her arm tightly!

"The next time I went to the chapel in the Galleries of Justice I was prepared for it. I was in control and I was provoking them! Whatever they threw at me I knew I could handle it. I'm a Wiccan, so I was drawing symbols on the floor, and to provoke

> *them I got the crucifix and cast it upside down on the symbols. My Wiccan faith was stronger this second time in the caves, and it enabled me to take them on."*

Liz believes that she was attacked by the spirits of long-dead Templar knights, and that these Templars could be responsible for the activity in the caves:

> *"Some of what happens in the Galleries is a haunting - actual spirits which think they own the place. The Templars in the caves think they own it. There are stories about the Templars in the past being in the caves under Nottingham. The caves predate the gaol, and are supposed to be linked to the caves under Nottingham Castle and most of the city. There were a lot of prisoners there, along with what you expect to find in prison – people who worked there, relatives, prisoners, victims of the Templars, the people they tortured. Dave [Ball] described seeing monk-like figures which could have been the Templars.*
>
> *"They are very, very strong because they had such a strong faith when they were alive, and when you*

> *believe in something so much it can sometimes leave the spirit energy to live on after physical death. They're not pleased when people are in the caves; when you go down there it can feel like walking into an argument, you can feel tension and an angry energy. When the Templars attacked me it wasn't because they are evil. They just wanted all of us out of the place."*

Liz was queried on her opinions on ghosts and explanations for what they could be. In relation to the apparitions at the Galleries of Justice and similar phenomena in different parts of the world, there are striking patterns – when people report seeing a ghost, they often describe a dark, cloaked figure that is shadowy and seems to glide along the ground. [10] This is true of apparitions glimpsed in the Galleries of Justice's caves and courtrooms, such as Simone's description of the apparition in the chapel.

Liz suggested that dark, cloaked figures are likely to be actual spirits, like the Templars, rather than residual energy or elementals. "My opinion is that if a person is taken or dies suddenly, the soul doesn't realise that the body is dead and it goes on as if in life," she explained.

---

[10] For examples, see the chapters on Dixie Dude Ranch, the Thing in the Cellar, Haunted Farmhouse by the Fjord, the Albrighton Apparition.

> *"There is energy animating the body, so where does it go after death? If the person has a strong will to exist, if there is a strong link to a person or a place, they want to stay there. That's a haunting. Dark figures are normally shy. They want to 'talk' but need encouraging. They're interested in us, and they come to see us, so they cover or hide themselves. Sensitives can see them in their cloaked state, catching a glimpse of them. Everyone is sensitive, people can sense if a room feels weird or something isn't right. Picking up on the atmosphere is the first sign that someone is sensitive, or has the potential to be sensitive. Paul [Dyason] started out as more of a sceptic, but now he picks up on stuff; he sees apparitions, he picks up on little things now he has more experience and has opened his mind up."*

She believes that some apparitions are disembodied spirits that are earthbound and have not passed on to whatever lies after death. They can become attached to a person or a place. They are intelligent, and can be seen by people, perhaps as shadowy, dark figures. Liz holds that they are responsible for poltergeist-type activity, such as throwing stones, moving objects and shutting or opening doors. However, it must be noted that there are many different opinions on the causes of paranormal activity; there is no definitive answer.

Some people feel that the paranormal activity at the Galleries of Justice and the caves in particular has been over-stated. "I like them," said Dawn, "but they're not as scary or haunted as people say they are. The place has been done to death. I think the spirits need a rest, they're probably sick of being asked to do stuff, which is why I think the place is becoming more flat now.

"The puking was like out of 'The Exorcist'"

Vanessa Penny has seen and heard plenty of things in the Galleries of Justice that defy this sense of ghostly weariness. Vanessa and Paul Dyason were pulled in all directions by outbreaks of unusual activity during a WOLF investigation at the Galleries. They were heading downstairs to place trigger objects – this is where objects are placed on paper with an outline drawn around them, in the hope that spirits will move them and show that they have been present.

Vanessa and Paul stopped in their tracks. They heard noises ahead. They knew no one else was down there. They could see a door had been opened which had previously been shut. Vanessa then heard doors slamming in the museum's women's quarters and then being stealthily opened. They were heading in this direction when they heard noises in the room they had just left.

"Paul is not normally scared, but he was this time!" Vanessa said. "As we were leaving we heard them again. Then we suddenly heard a horrible sound. It was like a man's last gasping breath, coming from the top of the stairs. I don't know what it was, I just ran off!"

There has been other trouble with doors mysteriously shutting at the Galleries of Justice. Liz Cormell was heading back to the crew-room (the 'base-camp') with a friend after a fag-break. "We passed a really heavy, old-fashioned door, with ornate glass panels," she said. "It was open, but as we went past it slammed hard shut. There was no one there to shut it and it didn't shut itself. We couldn't get it to happen again: we opened it and tried walking past, running past, jumping, everything, but we couldn't get it to shut. It was weird."

Sometimes it can be messy looking for ghosts at the Galleries of Justice, as attested by Rachel Penny. She related an incident where the spirits were guilty of causing a spot of nasty business:

> *"One time I was at an investigation with members of the public where a girl was puking. I wasn't there when it happened. She had been in the women's parlour or bedroom when she had become really nervous. She felt like energy had been zapped out of her. The puking was like out of*

'The Exorcist,' it was bad. Simone called Dave on the walkie-talkie and said she needed my help, as the girl was distraught.

"I was in the caves at the time, and had to go by myself through the dark. I had just got out of the tunnels and heading up the stairs when I heard footsteps behind me. They were heavy ones, going 'clump! clump! clump!'

"The noise was close to me. I thought someone was following me, and I looked behind me, pointing my torch. There was no one there – so I ran for it!"

Echoes of the Past:
Haunting at Occupation Street, Dudley

Interviews with Rachel Penny and Vanessa Penny

Even the quiet residential streets of Dudley cannot escape the claws of the paranormal. Beneath the respectable facade of Occupation Street are disturbances of a supernatural kind that tormented the Penny family for years.

Occupation Street is an ordinary, seemingly unremarkable place close to the centre of this Black Country town. It is near to Eve Hill and is located on the higher reaches of the Russell's Hall estate. It consists of two rows of early 20th century terraced housing, facing each other across a long road. Vanessa Penny has vivid memories of the street, having lived there with her family for several years. The strange activity began as soon as they moved in.

Vanessa is sensitive to the presence of spirits, and this ability was particularly sharp during the time she spent living at the property. She saw a number of entities. "There was an old woman who used to come along in visitation to the house," Vanessa said, "and she seemed to look after us. We actually got a death certificate showing that an old lady did die in the house. Her spirit is still there. I used to see a girl run up the stairs. Sometimes it was like a light moving along, other times more like an actual form. She had a white dress on and had blonde hair. She was short, about 4ft. It seemed like she was running from another spirit, a man that I saw."

Unlike the old woman and the girl, this man was not harmless or lacking threat. Vanessa felt that he was a malevolent presence in the house: "I didn't like him. He was not a nice ghost at all. He used to terrorise me. He would wake me up during the night, nudging me, and I would see him standing in the middle of the room or in the corner, looking at me. He had dark hair and wore something like a coal miner's jacket. Another time when I was asleep in my bedroom, I could feel something blowing in my ear, and then it was playing with my ear. I woke to see him right by me, right by my face."

Vanessa's sister Rachel experienced strange things at Occupation Street. She spent a month at the property sleeping on a sofa in the lounge, as she was between homes, and she did not sleep soundly.

"There was one night," Rachel said, "when I heard footsteps come all the way down the stairs and then across the backroom. I saw a shadow of someone moving. I was waiting for whoever it was to say something, as I thought it was my mom or Vanessa. But there was no one there. Another time I was half-asleep in the lounge and I heard loud footsteps. They were not a kid's!

"I knew something was in the house, and I knew Vanessa was telling the truth about what happened to her. I could feel the man's presence, but Vanessa could see him. I told her to protect herself and Mom. My mom is sensitive to stuff - the paranormal - like me and Vanessa, but she tries to block it off. In the house at Occupation Street she had hands come out of the wall and try to grab her."

The incidents continued for a long time. Eventually Vanessa and her family took action against the unwelcome intruders. They invited over three members of a local spiritualist church to investigate the problem. "These spiritualists used to stand at the front of the church, giving messages to people from their dead loved ones," Vanessa said. She hoped they could deal with whatever they found.

The atmosphere at Occupation Street changed in the hours before they arrived. It felt strange, and this worsened as the 'cleansing' of the property started.

The spiritualists were told nothing about the Penny family's experiences in the house, which allowed them to enter the property with open minds. They tried to divine what spirits were in the house – and their results suggested the girl and the dark man that Vanessa had encountered. These two spirits were apparently from the late 19th or early 20th century.

Rachel was also there to watch the cleansing, and was surprised that her dog Holly was scared: she whimpered and refused to go into the lounge or kitchen by herself, which was unlike Holly's normal behaviour.

"The spiritualists went around the house," said Vanessa, "blessing it and talking aloud, asking the spirits to leave, to go into the light. The spirit of the little girl went easy. They said they were then trying to get rid of the man, but he was a large energy, a right handful, and he had been taking energy from me. It took ages to get rid of him. It was hard work, much harder than the girl, because he didn't want to go. At one point he was pushed through the ceiling and they described him hanging halfway through, his legs dangling out."

This was pertinent to the explanation they later gave to Vanessa for the paranormal activity affecting Occupation Street.

"They told us that the house was crossed by ley lines and water lines," Vanessa explained. "They said that in the middle of the room downstairs this had created a vortex, a sort of opening that was bringing things into the house, like other ghosts. This was where the man had been dangling through the ceiling, and where there had been lots of activity."

This spiritual cleansing was successful. Vanessa and Rachel felt that the house was different, that the atmosphere had changed: it was friendlier and less oppressive. The girl and the dark man were gone. At least Vanessa could now sleep at night without being disturbed by curious men.

The one entity which remained was the old woman they thought had died in the house and whose spirit was protecting the family. The cleansing had been selective - not everyone had been turfed out.

Historical context

The site at Occupation Street has a surprisingly old history. Local library archives show that it is the probable location of the ancient manor of Russell's Hall – which gives its name to the modern residential estate.

The recorded history of the Russell's Hall manor begins in the 13th century, when the manor is likely to have received its name from the Russell family: the clan's headman, Johannes Russel, was named in records in c.1275 as the wealthiest man in Dudley. The manor passed into many different hands over the succeeding centuries: in the early 16th century, it was in the possession of Sir Thomas Boleyn, father of Anne Boleyn (the second wife of King Henry VIII and mother of Queen Elizabeth I). In the later 16th century, the manor house was a hiding place for holy relics – namely the bones of St. Chad, rescued from destruction at Lichfield Cathedral after the Reformation and kept for many years at Russell's Hall by recusant Catholics.

It must have looked very different compared to the dense housing and traffic that characterise modern Russell's Hall. Maps of 16th century Worcestershire show that the manor of Russell's Hall was a landmark for Dudley and the surrounding region; along with Dudley Castle they were the only two places of importance. Around the manor were more than thirty acres of arable land, with meadows and moorland; the landscape was littered with windmills, sheep and cows in pasture, and farmers on their plots. The manor house was demolished in 1844, after damage caused by mining operations beneath the ground. Paintings of the hall taken just before its demolition show a substantial building, with several tiers, a tower, a gatehouse and walls.

There is uncertainty over the original site of the manor house, or 'hall.' According to J.S. Roper, a historian who studied the historical maps of Dudley, the manor house was located at the northern, higher end of the Himley Road, very close to or on the site of what is now Occupation Street.[11] This was the second hall, built by Geoffrey Sutton, which stood between the 16th and 19th centuries. The original medieval hall may have been located at 'Old House Hill,' southwest of Himley Road and within Grange Park, adjacent to an old moor.

This long and chequered history gives a deeper meaning to the paranormal activity that occurred at Occupation Street. Many consider archaeology to be crucial in understanding ley lines, suggesting that they are the product of commonly- and well-travelled pathways and property markings.[12] Some might argue that land is made more psychically-resonant by the many centuries of habitation, all those years of humanity: the cycles of life and death, the emotions and tragedies of human life.

---

[11] "A History of Russell's Hall, Dudley," by J.S. Roper, 1973. This invaluable source gives much information on its early history.

[12] http://www.absoluteastronomy.com/topics/Ley_line

Perhaps the past existence of the ancient manor of Russell's Hall on the location of Occupation Street has created ley lines and the alleged 'vortex' which the spiritualists insisted passed through the property. The ghosts could have been echoes from the past; perhaps people seen through 'windows' in time and space; or even spiritual intruders from the past. The presence of holy relics at the manor house for many years could have had an impact, drawing mystical energies to the site.

All speculation, of course.

The Station Hotel

Brief history of hotel and an account of a WOLF paranormal investigation

Background

The Station Hotel opened in 1898. It is situated at the bottom of Castle Hill, in Dudley, which at the turn of the century was a relatively affluent part of the town. Across the road was the Opera House, a popular nightspot before it burned down in 1933, soon to be replaced by the Dudley Hippodrome. Some of the stars of the day performed at The Hippodrome, such as Bob Hope, Laurel & Hardy and George Formby, and they were among the luminary guests of the Station Hotel. It was a lively place – but expensive: most local contemporaries could not afford to pay for a drink in the hotel's then-highly fashionable bar, let alone pay for a room.

One of the gruesome stories that circulate around the hotel's hundred-odd year history is that of a murder. A lustful hotel manager enticed a serving girl into the cellar, hoping to have his way with her; when she spurned his advances and threatened to tell his wife, the girl was murdered. He strangled and stabbed her to death, then hid her body in a barrel.

This strongly corresponds with the information gained during one of the more eventful episodes of television's 'Most Haunted' series, when it used the Station Hotel as a location. Their psychic, Derek Acorah, picked up on a male spirit at the hotel with the name of George Williams or Williamson, who was having an affair with a female named Elizabeth Hitchen and later murdered her by strangulation and stabbing. Acorah learned that the body was removed from the hotel via a chute and buried near the front of the hotel, where it still lies undiscovered.

Among the spirits that Mr. Acorah sensed were a writer called George Lawley, who knew of the woman's murder (a person of this name was a local historian who worked as a writer for the brewery); several children who had died tragically; and a mysterious entity in the hotel's room 214 – the room where people have allegedly seen apparitions and been woken by them, and where the bed was filmed moving by itself by the 'Most Haunted' team.

Investigation

WOLF conducted an investigation at the Station Hotel in May 2008. The WOLF staff were in high spirits, and were hugely expectant. They knew the hotel's reputation.

The first part of the night was open to the public. Simone Taylor was with a group in the cellar, where they carried out glass divination, pendulum dowsing and séance experiments. The cellar seemed an 'active' part of the hotel. Vanessa Penny sensed a strange atmosphere here throughout the night, like something was waiting, watching them. The glass divination gave positive results: the glass tilted to one side and did a full circle on its rim a couple of times, after which there were small tapping noises, like pebbles being thrown. David Ball also experienced strange sensations while in the cellar, such as disorientation, pain in his back and something that felt like a graze on his knee. Once out of the cellar this disorientation and pain left David.

In the notorious room 214, a séance indicated the presence of a small girl, aged around five years and named Victoria. There was also a strong male energy that attempted communication.

Things were quiet in the rest of the hotel. In the restaurant and ball room, David picked up the energy of an elderly gentleman with "a big Edwardian tosh and smoking a pipe." It was largely hit and miss, and the investigation seemed to be ending in disappointment.

At around 3.30am the public event ended and most people left the hotel, with only the WOLF team members and associate members remaining behind. This consisted of Simone, David, Vanessa, Paul Dyason, Rachel Penny, Gemma Taylor and Julie Bennett.

It seemed that a switch had been flicked. The mood changed as they began their vigil in the hotel's cellar with a Ouija board session. "The cellar is renowned for having an entity down there," said Paul. "We were drawn there."

The next two hours stunned everyone, as Simone vividly described:

"The atmosphere at the time became extremely tense and apprehensive. The planchette did not seem to work too well so we swapped it to a glass on the Ouija board instead. We all had our fingers lightly on the glass with everyone at times letting go to verify nobody was influencing potential movement. We were aware of a female spirit named Mary; she was starting to communicate quite nicely but then everything seemed to change.

"The board itself started rotating underneath the glass! None of us could believe what we were seeing. It is all on film by the way![13]

"The board rotated 360 degrees one way and then completely full circle the other way, all with our fingers still on the glass. The board seemed to be moving all by itself. We were also asking out for noises, lights, and on countless occasions we all heard pebbles being thrown right beside us. I felt a sharp tug on the sleeve of my

---

[13] This footage can be viewed on YouTube. Follow the links:
http://www.youtube.com/watch?v=81cDiWc33hk
http://www.youtube.com/watch?v=fRhCsedJ9DQ&feature=related

t-shirt and became unnerved at the realisation that we were encountering something much more powerful than just spirits. We were all convinced the energy was elemental and purely negative.

"In periodic timings, the board would start to rotate again with the table moving side to side. Temperatures ranged dramatically: during one session of rotation, the temperature around the glass rose to 35 degrees, which was 10 degrees more than literally just a few seconds earlier. We could all feel a breeze around us and would report extreme cold feelings (confirmed by goosebumps) at the same time.

"One of the most memorable parts was the growl. We all heard deep breathing sounds. We all felt there was a build up and we were being tested. The movement of the board indicated that there was an attempt at getting us all to lose control of the glass and release whatever the energy was. I used a powerful Ouija ritual to close the session down and ensure our clean break from the

energy. [This was the typical 'White Light Protection Ritual.'] *Dave [Ball] instructed a protection ritual also.*

"We left the room after two hours, all startled, uneasy and shocked. In all the years of investigating there have been few experiences which have made me genuinely fearful for losing control of a situation and actually being scared - this was one of them!

"Sleeping in room 214 after this was like a walk in the park. By the time my head hit the pillow I'd almost forgot where I was through extreme tiredness and energy drainage."

The entity they encountered in the cellar was an elemental. These entities have been called demons or devils in the past, and Liz Cormell refers to them as living energy that is ancient, undying, and incredibly aware of the world. David described the elemental in the Station Hotel's cellar as a dark energy, having great supernatural intelligence and malevolent intentions; it desperately wanted to "get loose" of the Ouija board. The dangers of such an entity escaping its confines are discussed in the next chapter. They could include poltergeist activity or possession.

For Paul Dyason, it was one of the most extreme paranormal incidents he had witnessed with WOLF:

> *"I've never seen anything like it before. I still feel numb just thinking about it. The scariest thing for me was not so much the growl and breathing we all heard, nor the stones that were being flown about, but more so the potential of what this elemental entity could do if it got free of the board... It wanted to get loose by getting us to take a finger off. It distracted people by throwing stones, so that we would take a finger off. We had to keep going, so to close it properly, to keep control and stop it escaping from the board. Dave said it was close to manifesting... That really helped to concentrate the mind on what I was doing. It was an amazing couple of hours, after which I felt completely and utterly drained and exhausted."*

"That was one hell of a night!" David agreed.

The film footage of the séance in the cellar and the rotation of the Ouija board is amazing. It is impossible to fully discount the possibility that the board is being moved by the participants, as the room is dark and the shot is sometimes crowded with elbows and arms. Nevertheless the footage is very compelling. The Ouija board is moving by itself and makes more than one rotation before it stops, no one having touched it, and then it resumes its rotation. It turns one way and then the other. The glass is shown being touched by each person holding a single finger on it, and you can see that the amount of pressure being applied to the glass is gentle.

Evidence from the rest of the hotel is intriguing. Julie Bennett recorded what allegedly sounds like a voice on her digital recorder (which captures EVP, or Electronic Voice Phenomena) which speaks just after Simone asks the spirits a question; according to Julie it does not sound like anybody who was present at the time. Devices that record EVP can capture sounds that cannot be heard with normal hearing, and which are missed at the time.

There is also a photograph taken of the infamous room 214 which shows an unusual pair of orbs hovering over the bed. Orbs are normally small dots of light of varying size; there is an orb of this type in the photograph, but the other orb is like a trail of smoke that seems to lie across the bed. One person has said that it is like a head and a body, as if someone is lying or sitting on the bed.

Liz Cormell was not present at this investigation, but has visited the Station Hotel on other occasions:

> *"I felt something bad had happened down there in the cellar. I didn't like it all. It felt almost like being hunted.*

Now I know the story of the woman killed down there by the landlord, but I didn't know that at the time.

"I heard about the Ouija board spinning around at the Station Hotel. It's also happened at the Galleries of Justice and the Ram Inn. It's really, really weird. I don't know how someone could cheat, you'd see hands moving or feel the board being moved...I'm careful using Ouija boards in case of letting things out. Anything with the energy and the intelligence to move the planchette could be dangerous."

Ouija Boards:
Perilous Gateways into the Unknown

An essential tool of paranormal investigation is the Ouija board. This method of spirit communication has been used for making contact with non-corporeal entities for perhaps thousands of years, and is now commonly used at haunted locations.

What is a Ouija board?

Modern Ouija boards are usually flat boards marked with the letters of the alphabet, the numbers zero to nine, and the words 'yes' and 'no.' It is used for communication with entities from astral worlds by asking them to move a 'planchette' (literally a pointer, perhaps a triangular heart-shaped piece of wood with a central glass panel, or a glass of some sort) to spell out or indicate their message.

The communication happens during a séance, in which participants each place a finger on the planchette. This could possibly 'power' the planchette by linking it to their electro-magnetic currents or 'life-force.' Some people like to begin by saying a prayer to God, or to their guardian angel or spirit guide, asking for spiritual protection. One person usually takes the lead in asking questions, progressing from 'yes/no' to more complex questions. Others can join in asking questions. Results are not always immediate: success requires time and practice.

It has become usual to ask for any spirits that are close-by to make themselves known, and to give their message by moving the planchette to indicate their message – "Is there anyone there?" for example. However, as discussed later, some experts consider this to be quite dangerous. These simple words are magical commands that summon the _closest_ entity, not always the most appropriate or helpful entity. Questions such as "When am I going to die?" are best avoided. Pertinent, careful questions are better. There is advice against asking for the entity to cause physical phenomenon, such as throwing stones or knocking tables and walls, as this request for it to move from beyond the restraints of its astral dimension into our physical world through the portal of the Ouija board could be hazardous if there are not proper controls.

To end the session safely, the spirits should be thanked for their help and bade goodbye; only when the planchette is moved by the entity to indicate goodbye should the glass be removed. If the spirit is reluctant to do this, the users should firmly say something along the lines of, "Goodbye and leave," and then quickly take their fingers off the planchette. This is just one of many different methods for ending a session.

Any person wishing to experiment with a Ouija board is strongly advised to research how to handle a session safely.

A very short history of Ouija boards

Similar 'spirit boards' have been around for a long time. They were used in Ancient Greece and Rome, with 'Fuji' or 'planchette writing' used in Ancient China in c.1100 B.C. Some tribes of American Indians used spirit boards. Ouija boards as we know them in the modern western world entered the mainstream of popular consciousness in the late 19th century, when they were used as divining tools by spiritualists. In recent decades they have been showcased in films and television programmes, usually as a plot device for bringing supernatural evil into our physical world.

Explanations and scepticism

It has been argued that the movement of the planchette is caused by a physical condition called the 'ideomotor effect':

> *"The ideomotor effect is a psychological phenomenon wherein a subject makes motions unconsciously. As in reflexive responses to pain, the body sometimes reacts reflexively to ideas alone without the person consciously deciding to take action. For instance, tears are produced by the body unconsciously in reaction to powerful emotions. Automatic writing, dowsing, facilitated communication, and Ouija boards have also been*

> *attributed to the effect of this phenomenon. Mystics have often attributed this motion to paranormal or supernatural force. Many subjects are unconvinced that their actions are originating solely from within themselves."*[14]

It is possible that the movement of the planchette is caused by the strain of maintaining the finger's grip on the planchette: if the arm has been kept up for some time, the tiredness produced might cause slight, unintended movements. A more sceptical explanation is that one or more participants 'cheat' by consciously and surreptitiously moving the planchette to give a particular message. "I'm never 100% certain people are not pushing it themselves," said Dawn Goding.

"They're good tools if the right people are using them," said Simone Taylor, "but you can probably discount 95% of things said through Ouija boards."

Scepticism must be undermined somewhat in light of the many accounts of sessions that have revealed information no participant could have known and which has been verified afterwards. One such instance is Simone's encounter with a self-confessed murderer during a Ouija board session.[15] A séance held by WOLF at the Station Hotel's cellar is another compelling

---

[14] http://en.wikipedia.org/wiki/Ideomotor_effect

[15] See page 113

argument in favour of the Ouija board's authenticity. The actual board was moving in answer to their questions, not the planchette.[16] "When we were using the Ouija board, the glass was moving violently," said Rachel Penny, "Then the board started twizzling like mad while our fingers were still on the glass."

Simone Taylor concurs with Rachel: "The planchette wasn't moving, it was the actual board. It was twisting all the way round in one direction, going as far as it could without people losing their grip on the planchette; then it would twist all the other way round again. There was no explanation for it. We tried replicating it afterwards, but we couldn't make it happen."

This was recorded on camera and can be viewed on YouTube.[17]

Perils to sanity and soul

Ouija boards are potentially dangerous, whether they are genuine tools for spirit communication or not. The damage to a person with a fragile psychological or emotional condition can be immense. It must be terrifying to believe that some random spiritual creature wishes to hurt you or even just talk to you. It can be so frightening that it causes paranoia or schizophrenic episodes.

---

[16] See page 64

[17] Ibid

Hans Holzer, a pioneering paranormal researcher, said that spirits contacted through a Ouija board can become obsessed with the person or people who called them.[18] He drew attention to the case of a woman who, through using a Ouija board, had made contact with a spirit that claimed to be a deceased ex-lover. It started talking to her in her mind, and would not stop even after the Ouija board had been thrown away. It refused to leave her.[19] Whether this was the result of mental illness or an actual encounter with a perverse spirit, it shows that Ouija boards can be dangerous.

Experts who believe in the power of Ouija boards give strong advice against their irresponsible use. In a recent book, J. Edward Cornelious warns that if a participant in a Ouija board séance calls out blindly and randomly for spirits (i.e. "Is anyone there?"), they are making open invitations to whatever entities are out there.[20] He argues that there is no conscious control over what is being channeled. There is the chance of coming into contact with elementals, rather than spirits. These elementals are not human, and have never been human, and exist in other dimensions or astral planes. They have been referred to as demons and fairies in past history. They are infinitely malleable and able to transform their

---

[18] Hans Holzer's most famous investigation was the 'Amityville Horror' case in 1977.

[19] For further information on this case, see 'The Greenhaven Encyclopaedia of Paranormal Phenomena,' by Patricia D. Netzley, 2006

[20] J. Edward Cornelious, *Aleister Crowley and the Ouija Board*, 2005

appearance and language, to dress themselves in people's mental imagery, including memories – to be what people *want* them to be. They can convincingly impersonate deceased people.

This does not necessarily discount the chance of genuine, disincarnated spirits coming to the Ouija board, though it is difficult to communicate with the dead if their souls have reincarnated or in some irretrievable way 'passed on.' Some people do not believe that Ouija boards can communicate with ghosts, as they cannot tap into the psychic residue left by severe emotional events (replayed in future time and space as ghostly disturbances) as it cannot 'talk' back.

Elementals that have escaped from Ouija boards are associated by paranormal specialists with hauntings, poltergeists and possessions. They can turn on the people that summon them and trick their way to freedom. Often they are unwittingly left free to escape by people with no idea of safety procedures for a Ouija board. If let-loose, elementals can be responsible for knocks and rappings, drafts, cold spots and moving of objects – all the phenomenon associated with a poltergeist.

Vanessa Penny's family discovered a Ouija board at a house they moved into in Dudley.[21] She believes it had

---

[21] This is not the property at Occupation Street discussed in a previous chapter

been used by a previous occupant who had been irresponsible in their communications with spirits:

> *"They let something stay in the house that wasn't sent back after being called upon. One night I was at the bathroom at the top of the stairs, heading to the toilet, and I looked down. There was someone at the bottom staring at me. It was horrible! I saw a monk, with a black cloak. It was an evil presence. I used to feel like I was being watched. When we were watching TV sometimes one of us sensed something by our shoulder, looking at us. Dogs used to go mad. My dad used to keep the lights on when he was watching TV, because he was anxious, and this was a man who was in the army! Everyone moves out within a few years, it's always up for sale."*

The ultimate scare-story is 'The Exorcist,' a book (adapted into a film) that spawned much fear about Ouija boards after showing a girl possessed by a demon after playing with a Ouija board. 'The Exorcist' is based on a supposedly true story of a young boy in St. Louis, U.S.A., circa 1949, who was taught to use Ouija boards by an aunt obsessed with the occult. After she died, the boy used a Ouija board she had left him. Poltergeist-type incidents soon began happening at the boy's home: his bed would shake, furniture moved by itself, and there was unexplained scratching on the walls. This culminated in his demonic possession and an exorcism that lasted thirty-odd days.

Ouija boards are considered to be safer if proper guidelines are followed: such as avoiding using a Ouija board alone; using boards in comfortable environments; using boards with trusted people, and avoiding the mentally or emotionally unstable; and beginning and ending a séance involving a Ouija board properly, lest spiritual entities are allowed to roam free. Fingers must remain on the planchette no matter what, until the session is formally and safely ended, and the entity is sent back. Taking a finger off the planchette is like opening a hole for it to escape through. The entities should be summoned by name, and commanded to remain in this portal throughout the séance. J. Edward Cornelious encourages the use of specialist techniques, incantations and ceremonial dress.[22]

---

[22] See J. Edward Cornelious, *Aleister Crowley and the Ouija Board*, 2005

The Haunted Hospital

Personal account of a WOLF paranormal investigation

Hospitals are never nice places. Sick people are sent there; these people often suffer from extreme pain or humiliation as their bodies buckle and break down, before yielding to death. Hospitals are inextricably linked with the passing of life. A desolate hospital, long since closed for use and sheared of all furnishings or equipment or staff, would provide haunting-substance enough for any paranormal investigator.

WOLF was invited to an unnamed hospital that had shut its doors. It was clarified that any investigation was to be conducted in the strictest confidence, with the location remaining unidentified. The hospital had an impressive history of supernatural activity, of which WOLF was keenly aware.

The WOLF team members who attended the investigation were: Simone Taylor, David Ball, Vanessa Penny, Rachel Penny, Paul Dyason, and Liz Cormell. Associate members who attended the investigation were Kevin Berrill, Julie Bennett and Dawn Goding. I joined the early tour of the hospital as an observer, before leaving prior to the vigil held later that night.

"I had this feeling that something wasn't right"

The hospital's weird ambience and empty corridors could not fail to remind me of horror film clichés, specifically 'Halloween II,' where nurses are stalked and murdered by a juggernaut maniac. Dave also referred to scenes from 'The Frighteners,' where a murderous ghost hunts down his prey in a derelict hospital. The location was richly evocative of all these scenes of horror.

What struck me was the sheer labyrinthine character of the hospital. The place was so large and dark, with the only lighting coming from external streetlights. Long murky corridors seemed to spout rooms and twist into new passageways. It was abandoned - like the Mary Celeste - with no one manning the ship. There was little or no décor, only crumbling plasterwork and debris; this was disorientating, as it was difficult to recognise where one was. It made it so easy to become lost.

Kevin felt positive at the start of the night's investigation and echoed my own feelings. "On initially walking into the hospital I felt fine," he said, "no worries at all and no foreboding of the night ahead."

During this preliminary search, several investigators were disturbed by weird sounds in the corridors. There were reports of vague footsteps or thuds. Not far from the conference room – where a vigil was held later – the entire group halted at a large open area where several corridors crossed. Simone was the first to halt, as she thought she saw a shadow flit across the wall. I could see weird shadows on the same spot, almost like people rushing past, but I concluded that they were cast by the branches of trees swaying in the wind outside.

Even so, I could swear that I heard a gentle throbbing noise filling the air. It was low, not loud at all, it seemed far away; and everyone strained to listen to it. Perhaps it was background noise, or mere silence amplified into something meaningful by our concentrated attempts to listen to it.

"We continued down corridor after corridor," said Kevin, "many of which were fine but some really put me on edge. What it was I don't know, I just seemed to have this feeling that something wasn't right, and I went goose-pimperly from head to toe."

The tour took us to a swimming pool area. The pool was obviously empty of water, and the room was bare. There was no real energy here. Vanessa and I heard bangs; I thought I heard a pipe moving or being tapped in the distance.

For a short time we split into two smaller groups. One WOLF team close to the hospital wards reported that they had heard footsteps where there were no other people. They had been in a corridor, listening to the clear noise of sets of footsteps moving across rooms above them and walking down stairs loudly, advancing down the corridor towards them before slowly disappearing. They had seen nothing to explain the footsteps, and the other team was apparently not in this area at that time. However, I do consider that it might have been caused by people in other parts of the hospital, which has many winding passageways and concealed stairways. It is sometimes difficult to know at what exact position in the building you are standing, especially in the dark, or in which direction to find other people.

"I could feel the table vibrating underneath my hands"

The first big vigil of the night was held in a meeting room. I was sceptical of this room's history of paranormal activity: in previous years, before the hospital's closure, my job saw me attending meetings in this same room and I was sometimes here by myself for quite a while. I cannot remember ever sensing anything unusual. The hospital was not stripped and empty in those bright daylight hours, so perhaps I am being harsh.

The nine investigators participated in table-tipping on the room's dominating boardroom table. They were positioned in an energy-raising circle. Communication with spirits took place, with the formula of one knock for yes, two for no. There was nothing dramatic at first. Simone took temperature readings in the room at intervals, and they never changed from 18°c despite several people reporting coldness across their hands. Rachel was startled by the sensation of something grabbing her leg.

The heavy-oak table seemed to be faintly vibrating. The investigators could feel this with their fingertips lightly touching it. There was a delicate tremor go through the table, followed by a number of sudden loud bangs near where Paul was standing. They seemed to occur in answer to questions. "We were all quite amazed at the volume and distinctness of these knocks," said Paul, "so we all deliberately stepped as far back from the table as we could while maintaining our fingertips on the edge. I then mentioned to the group that I was feeling a chest pain."

Vanessa also experienced sharp pains in her chest at this point. They were unaware that a person was supposed to have died of a heart-related problem in the same room. Vanessa's chest was tight and it felt like she could not breathe; psychically she felt that someone had suffered a heart attack in the room, and the name 'Michael' came to her. In later communication with spirits, Liz was told that a male energy tied to the location had died of a stroke in the room.

There did not seem to be any unusual temperatures or EMF (electro-magnetic field) readings around Paul, Rachel and Vanessa. People swapped places around the table and everyone placed their hands flat on the table to reduce the possibility of unknowingly distributing their weight badly and thereby creating noises. Yet the bangs continued. Some people felt them coming from directly beneath their hands, which was very unnerving. "I could feel the table vibrating underneath my hands when the taps came," Rachel said. "We had this happen for a good hour in this room."

Simone reported that the table appeared to be vibrating continually, and remarked on the eerie atmosphere: "Throughout the entire vigil in this area, all investigators commented on the regular bangs, sounds of footsteps and feelings that something was going on in the corridor area." Vanessa and Rachel heard noises like shuffling, rustles and footsteps near the meeting room on a number of occasions, which sounded almost like people walking past.

An unhinged, heavy door that was near to the meeting room was repeatedly found shut by Rachel and Kevin prior to the séance, despite being left open by them on the occasions they passed through it. The opposite thing happened after the séance in the meeting room, when it was found open even though they had seen it was shut. They had observed no one go past during the interval. Considering it was off its hinge at the top and the frame was almost out of the wall, the door would have probably been very noisy to open. According to Kevin, it could not have shut by itself, as it had to be physically moved, which caused loud scraping across the floor.

"Dave started to freak out about the black dog"

The WOLF team decided to hold a vigil in the hospital's notorious wards. One ward in particular seemed more repellent than the others did. During the tour I smelt something disgusting in the area; I suppose it could have been a very rotten patch of damp. I saw that a few investigators had goose pimples in this ward, where as they did not before.

They experimented with using Dave as a trigger object: he dressed in a patient's gown found earlier that night, and sat on the floor while the rest of the team sat against the opposite wall. "For the comical value alone we knew this would be a memorable vigil," said Simone, "and we were conscious that laughter is allegedly a good source for increasing energy levels, so it was not necessarily a misplaced factor."

Dave began calling out for a nurse or for matron to help him, pretending that he had fallen out of bed and ringing a bell brought along as an additional trigger object. Other investigators also called out. This seemed to be successful at stimulating paranormal activity – the team heard a succession of taps and bangs, and Dave excitedly sat up when he saw a figure that appeared as a light anomaly go right past him towards the adjacent operating theatre. No one else saw this, and few seemed to feel anything potent in the atmosphere. Simone was surprised at her temperature readings, which showed a higher reading to the right of Dave – this was 21°c, rather than the 18°c found elsewhere, and the higher temperature spread to around 4ft beyond him.

There was a sudden change of tempo, as the supernatural energies quickened. Dave called out for a spirit to interact and show itself. The group was aware of what sounded like a female voice whispering to them from somewhere close by. The words were not clear.

The WOLF investigators decided to form a circle around Dave by linking hands. They performed a séance.

Simone was clear on the reasons for this: "The theory is that if the spirit was thinking she had a patient to deal with in the hospital, the energy from the circle may enable her to manifest herself. I asked the group to link hands and feel the protecting energy flow through everyone and specifically from left to right, the direction being significant as it is like opening a bottle of pop, allowing access from the spirit world."

There were unexpected results. Dave felt a surge of overwhelming fear and stood bolt upright in panic - in the words of Rachel he "freaked out" – as he saw a large black dog enter the room. He watched it walk around the corner into the ward and look straight at the group, before turning back and leaving the same way.

This was allegedly a 'phantom' black dog, the tradition of which pre-dates the Middle Ages. They are sometimes considered to be protective creatures, but more usually feared as an omen of death and misfortune, and potentially demonic in origin.

"I was cold to the bone, I couldn't stop shaking"

When asked, Dave could not be sure if it was a domestic animal or something more sinister. He was becoming increasingly uncomfortable and worried that they had conjured up something dangerous. He said that black dogs are often "gatekeepers" for other entities. They had to be careful.

The group was divided. Liz quickly advised that they needed to leave the area immediately for their own protection, but concurred with Dave that breaking the circle would remove their psychic defence from whatever spirits were in the room. Others felt that it was pointless to run from the very thing they were trying to contact.

Simone looked across to where Dave had seen the black dog and was shocked to see a pair of yellow eyes staring back at her. She told the others, who suggested that yellow eyes were better than red, as black dogs with red eyes are considered to be demonic. Kevin now started to shake uncontrollably and began to have breathing difficulties. Alarm at the black dog was creating hysteria.

Kevin stood in the circle as belongings were picked up, the circle manoeuvring so that it was never broken or its protection disrupted. The decision was made to end the vigil before anything terrible happened.

The WOLF investigators were worse for wear upon returning to base. Liz told the group that they had been under psychic attack in that ward, and she was feeling very poorly after exiting the vigil.

"That was the weirdest feeling I've ever had," said Kevin, who was shook up by his experience. "I don't know what happened to me. I went really cold, as if I was standing in cold water; I was cold right to the bone. I couldn't stop shaking, my head was spinning. I didn't feel good. It took me a little while to get over my experience."

"I was caught with my pants down"

The rest of the night's investigation never hit the same heights. The WOLF investigators braved the hospital ward again in hope of gathering further evidence, but its super-charged atmosphere had dissipated - it was lighter and not so heavy with dread. A séance produced no further activity, though Paul and Dawn both commented on the sensation of sharp stabbing pains in the necks and backs. After the group moved their vigil into the adjoining operating theatre, investigators could hear small indistinct thuds and bangs from the ward, for which they had no proper explanation. By 5am, the investigation had reached its natural end.

"I think the bit that got me the most was seeing that black dog," David said. "I don't ever want to see that again, I truly felt I was caught with my pants down on that one."

"It was a great night with everything we heard," said Julie, "from the muffled voices, doors banging, knocks on tables, tapping and doors opening and closing by themselves – not to mention the evil black dog! I think it's definitely worth another visit if we get the chance. Maybe Dave can get himself a doctor's outfit next time and dress up for us again."

I am unsure in my judgement on the paranormal activity reported during the night's investigation. The hospital certainly has a gloomy character during the hours of darkness, and the morass of empty corridors can be unsettling. Nevertheless, I am familiar with the experiences of nurses on night shifts: the eeriness of hospitals with a near-total absence of people, in contrast to the bustling daytime hours. What we experienced was not unusual. The phenomenon experienced by WOLF might be attributed to many things: to echoes of investigators' own footfall; sensory deprivation and disorientation; inadvertent hand movements during table tipping; or hysteria during the black dog incident.

I did not witness the thuds on the meeting room table nor the black dog stalking the WOLF team, so I cannot offer the incidents a personal appraisal. I can only admit that the old haunted hospital is an especially unique place. I did not find it relaxing or comfortable. It did not make me feel welcome.

Haunting at Withymoor

Interviews with Helen Taylor and Simone Taylor

It seemed just an ordinary day when Helen Taylor came home from work. She went upstairs, and tried to open the bathroom door. It would not shift open. It was held fast against her. This was frightening stuff for Helen: "It was like someone was behind it. It was only open a bit. I pushed and pushed till eventually it slammed open. I was scared stiff and ran downstairs and shut myself in the kitchen."

When her husband, David Taylor, came home soon afterwards he put his front door key into the lock. The door moved slightly but became stuck after just a few inches. It was just like the bathroom door. David knew something was wrong. He pushed the door, and put his full strength into it, but it would not budge. He thought Helen was braced against it somehow on the other side, and he shouted through the letter-box, screaming at her to stop holding the door and to let him in. David desperately flung himself against the door.

"It slammed open," said Helen. Whatever force had prevented the door from opening was suddenly gone as it flung on its hinges, showing that no one had been behind the door. David rushed into the house. "He came to the kitchen and saw me," Helen continued. "I was terrified. Then he went upstairs with a knife."

They searched the house but found no intruders. There was no rational explanation for this bizarre incident.

It seemed to fit in with Helen's belief that the house at Penfield's Road, Withymoor, was haunted. There were other events that confirmed to her that it was inhabited by a supernatural entity: "I was awoken by someone standing at the bottom of the bed," she said. "It moved next to me. He was tall and in a black hooded cape. I put my hand out and my hand went through him. I screamed and woke Dave and it disappeared. We sometimes smelled clan tobacco in the house, and mostly on the landing. It was a smell that I will never forget."

David Taylor is a whole-hearted sceptic on all things paranormal, but even he has no way to explain the phenomenon that occurred at the house in Withymoor Village estate, near Stourbridge, in the West Midlands. It was a new-build property, and they were the first people to live there. There have been several phases of construction in this large estate of detached and semi-detached housing: the first houses were built between 1971 and 1978, primarily on the site of former collieries, scrapyards and farmland, with some later developments on the site of the former William Kings Brick Works. There have been problems with subsidence at Withymoor: several houses are supposed to have structural underpinning, and some have been demolished after safety fears.

The presence of mining activity and tunnels under parts of Withymoor might explain sightings of miner's ghosts by several local residents. This has typically occurred at night, when people have been in their bedrooms.

Their daughter's interest in the paranormal might have originated in this eerie house. "I distinctly remember (as crazy as it sounds) flying down the stairs," said Simone Taylor. "Well, more like floating down, as I remember the feeling of gentleness. My mom said I used to say it all the time. I was three years old." Something must have carried her down the stairs.

Simone has personal recollections of a clown that lived in her bedroom, or what she thought was a clown: "Now I'm older I believe it to possibly be the same spirit that my mom saw, but through a child's eyes...There was something there, and it was not something nice. It used to scare me."

She believes that she used the image of a clown to mask what was actually there, as a defensive technique, hoping to make it seem safer and less dangerous so she could cope with the fear she felt. She drew upon imagery that existed in her sub-conscious, and feels that many paranormal entities receive their shape or appearance from images with which people are familiar. This could be why people can see such a range of different things when they encounter the supernatural. It also fits in with the notion of elementals as trickster entities that can later their form and appearance.

The Albrighton Apparition

Interview with Alex (pseudonym)

Alex is a psychology student living in the West Midlands. When he was younger, his family lived in Albrighton, Shropshire; this large village is near the city of Wolverhampton and RAF Cosford, and pre-dates the Domesday Book. One of the biggest shocks of Alex's childhood came when he was just six years old. "It's the only time I've been sure that I've seen a ghost," he said.

The family house was a sturdy, old-fashioned terraced-type property built in the 1890s. Alex shared an upstairs bedroom with his older brother. Restless and unable to sleep one night, he played quietly with his toys into the early hours. The house was still. Alex needed the toilet and went to the bedroom door. He opened it. Standing outside at the doorway was a towering apparition.

"It was a hooded figure," said Alex, "tall, maybe around 6 foot or so, wearing a brown cloak. It had glowing white eyes, like glowing stars, set into a black shadowy face. I couldn't make out the features. It stood exactly still, very close, one or two feet away from me. It was looking down at me, the eyes looking at me, like white disks of light.

"It was like a very tall Jawa from 'Star Wars.'

"I was too frightened to scream. I had an eerie feeling, it felt strange. It wasn't harmful. The scariest thing about it was the silence."

The whole experience lasted for around ten seconds, until Alex shut the door out of fright. He cannot remember if he then tried to wake up his brother, or whether he hid under his bedcovers and eventually went to sleep. Over the next few days, Alex was terrified that he would see it again. He never did. But after this encounter with a ghostly apparition, he was always afraid to go upstairs at the house, especially at nighttime.

Haunting at Coseley

Interviews with Liz Cormell and Rachel Penny

Rachel Penny moved into a flat in Coseley, West Midlands, at a stressful time in her life. She had experienced a traumatic break-up with her long-term boyfriend, losing some belongings as she was forced to look for somewhere else to live. Her new flat then needed gutting and redecorating. She was also changing jobs.

At this same time, strange incidents were bedevilling her family in their house at Occupation Street, Dudley, and Rachel had a few peculiar experiences during the few nights that she stayed there.[23] This outburst of supernatural activity must have cast a shadow over Rachel's life in her new flat.

"I sensed something was wrong as soon as I moved in," she said. "At times it would suddenly seem as if the light had been drowned out. The colour in the room would go, and it seemed sort-of misty. Ornaments would get moved: my dogs on the television always face in the same direction, but when I came back one day they had all been turned to face the other direction. No one had been in the house; I didn't know how it could have happened. Another time my sofa was pushed back, I could see the marks on the carpet from where it was

---

[23] See pages 55-56

normally. Sometimes when watching TV I could see something out of the corner of my eye in the doorway. My dog would stare at the doorway too."

Her dog Holly did not like living at the flat and was barking more than usual. Rachel was becoming less comfortable. She reported cold spots in the flat and vile smells that she could not explain; she was surprised to find orbs [i.e. spirit energies in the form of light anomalies] in photographs she had taken in two rooms of the flat. More unsettling was the sensation that unseen eyes were watching her.

When Liz Cormell visited Rachel's flat, she sensed the spirit of a girl playing hide and seek behind the sofa, though she could not pick up on exactly who she was. Rachel also had a notion that the spirit of an old lady was in the kitchen, but that something else in the flat was causing all the trouble.

Just before Christmas, Rachel came into contact with Sandrea Mosses, a medium who was working at Wolverhampton Spiritualist Church. They met when Rachel had a one-to-one reading with her, after Sandrea was recommended by a work colleague. She invited the medium and her colleague Martin to the flat, hoping they could help. They asked Rachel if she could wait in her car and leave them alone in the property for a short while, for her own safety. "Her vulnerability and her inexperience made her an easy target," said Sandrea.

In her report of the incident, Sandrea sensed a dark entity in the property, a male who entered through the living room.[24] As they started 'clearing' or 'cleansing' the flat, she sensed it disliked Martin but wanted to dominate her, because she was a female. It knew what they intended to do, to get rid of him.

"He was quite happy in his current environment and had no intention of going anywhere," said Sandrea. "This dark entity did not want to leave this world. He had lived a life of debauchery. Excessive drinks and drugs were a way of life for him during his time on earth. He couldn't resist displaying his involvement with young teenage girls, who hung around his flat and were obviously being exposed to things young girls of their age should not have seen."

To trick the entity into exposing itself they offered Martin as a vessel for it to enter. The temptation was too great for it to resist and it took the bait. Martin started to 'transfigure,' to physically change in appearance: stubble was suddenly showing on his face, the jaw was squarer, and he seemed taller.

As it began exerting more influence on Martin, Sandrea's spiritual helpers came into play – in particular the spirit of an American Indian. "I saw in my mind's eye a huge feathered wing sweep through Martin and magic the being away," said Sandrea. In a blink of the eye, Martin returned to his usual self, and his energy reverted back to his own. In the space of an hour, the dark entity had been driven out of the flat.

---

[24] Sandrea Mosses, *Spheres of an Unseen World*, 2009

"As soon as Rachel walked in, she immediately commented on the difference in the whole feel of the flat. The sinister feeling was no longer present. The flat remained clear and to this day she has had no further problems."

Rachel agreed that after Sandrea's visit the flat no longer felt unpleasant or malevolent. "I could see the difference," she said. "It wasn't so dark or misty anymore. Things have been okay since then.

"Sandrea told me that the dark entity was the spirit of a drug dealer that would walk through the flats where I live. It was linked to the area before it was flats, back to the 1960s, when there used to be a path along where the flats are now. There are ley lines running along it, too; spirits and energies use it as a path, as ley lines are energy lines - spirits move along them. There's also a church nearby."

Surprisingly, Rachel is still not alone in the flat. There is more keeping her company on windswept evenings than just her pet dog, Holly. There is another entity at the flats, a man walking along a corridor that Rachel has sometimes seen out of the corner of her eye, shadowy and creeping. Liz Cormell, a medium for WOLF, has suggested that this is a residual energy, rather than a haunting by a spirit. After the cleansing, Rachel was told that the old lady in the kitchen was her grandmother, who was there trying to protect her.

Sandrea informed her that the spirit of the girl that Rachel and Liz encountered playing in the flat was actually Rachel's daughter, who seemed to be around eight or nine years old. This was a shock, as Rachel has never had children; but she feels that it could be a child from a miscarriage. "The dates could be right," said Rachel. "There's no way to tell. The girl was left here in the bedroom but she's okay, she comes and goes."

The Ancient Ram Inn

Interviews with Liz Cormell, Paul Dyason, Dawn Goding, Rachel Penny and Simone Taylor

The Ancient Ram Inn is considered to be one of the most haunted places in Britain. A former pub and Grade II listed building in Wotton-under-Edge (Gloucestershire) it has an extremely long and less-than venerable history. It is reputably built on the site of a 5,000 year old pagan burial ground, and dates from around the mid-12th century. It was originally a church or chapel, with a sideline in brewing, and perhaps by as early as 1350 it had become an inn. Now it survives as a ramshackle relic, with uneven stone walls and decayed windows. The rooms heave with junk and antiques, and can be very, very cold.

Over the centuries there have been well-substantiated accounts of murders at the Ram Inn, along with rumours of satanic worship, black magic and ritual sacrifice of children. A huge number of ghosts and spirits have been catalogued at the Ram Inn by paranormal investigators. Several are supposed to be malevolent and aggressive, and want to strangle people. There is a witch that wants to hurt people; an incubus and a succubus, demons or evil spirits that sneak into people's beds when they are asleep for sexual intercourse; ghostly cats and dogs; ghostly children, highwaymen, and prostitutes; spirits of genteel ladies who were murdered; and ex-landlords of the pub, whose spirits have not left.[25] It must be a very crowded place.

There have been dramatic investigations at the Ancient Ram Inn by paranormal groups in recent years, and it gained further notoriety after the 'Most Haunted' television series filmed there.

The apparition in the doorway

WOLF have encountered unnerving phenomenon during their investigations at this location. There was a remarkable sighting of an apparition in the barn, witnessed by around twenty to thirty people including the WOLF staff. This was part of an investigation open to the public, who were encouraged to participate in the search for paranormal activity. The lights were off as the group was conducting a psychic circle. The barn covers a large area, and at one end is a double doorway. The group heard noises in this direction and turned to look. In the doorway they saw what Liz Cormell describes as "the shadow of a man standing there, leaning forwards with his hands on his knees."

Everybody seems to have seen it. Simone saw this outline of a figure standing in the doorway, which she says disappeared after torches were pointed at it. The lights were put back on and there was no one standing there. This same apparition seems to have been spotted

---

[25] For further information on its history, please refer to http://www.theancientraminn.com.

on two or more occasions by visitors, making it more impressive.

Strange things in the bar

The bar area is another paranormally-active part of the Ram Inn. Stories of tunnels running from the bar's fireplace would suggest the influence of ley lines, as the Ram Inn is built on the crossing of two lines.

Dawn Goding has seen footage of the bar recorded by another paranormal organisation on old-fashioned video film. It seems to show a person appearing and then disappearing: the camera operator is panning around the bar, past the fireplace and then coming back around, all taking around 15 seconds; the footage seems to show a person leaning back in a chair in front of the fireplace, then on the return shot they are gone. There was not supposed to be any one else in the bar at that time.

Dawn also discussed a sound recorded during a WOLF investigation that they could not fully explain: "We were sitting in the bar by the fireplace. The sound was like a slow creaking of a door – or maybe a very long, quiet fart. An old lady in her eighties was near where the noise came from and she was adamant it wasn't her farting. She completely denies it to this day."

Liz Cormell was in the bar's snug during a vigil involving psychic circles and Ouija boards. She was drawn to the fireplace for some reason, sensing that something was there. The bar was quiet. The small group heard someone walk down the stairs and through the bar, and a woman sitting closest to the snug's exit to the bar saw a man walk through. She thought it was David Ball.

Then David came walking into the bar from a completely different direction. He had heard footsteps and come from another part of the building to investigate. "The woman couldn't believe it," said Liz. "The man who'd walked through couldn't have been Dave and there was no one else in the area. She was totally gobsmacked."

This event was verified by other groups working at the Ancient Ram Inn at the same time. Paul Dyason recollects the sounds of someone walking down the stairs from near the 'bishop's room.' He called out but there was no answer, and when he went to look there was no one there. A group upstairs in the 'witch's bedroom' had heard the footsteps at the same time as Paul and the group in the bar. "The footsteps had a good logical path," Paul said, "from upstairs, downwards and to the bar."

Knocking on the bishop's bed

The bishop's room is a frightening part of the Ancient Ram Inn. Several of the more malignant, hostile spirits are said to frequent the bishop's room, alongside more protective entities. It is conjectured that there is a remnant here from the Inn's previous incarnation as a church - some sort of religious man. It has been suggested that there is more than one such spirit here, after people have reported seeing a bishop, a monk and a priest among others; it could perhaps be a single spirit whose appearance has been perceived differently.

An awesomely peculiar object appeared to David and Paul on one occasion when they were staying overnight in the bishop's room. "We were beginning to wind-down for sleep," said Paul, "when Dave asked, "Can you see this?!" He was pointing to something. I saw it, it was bizarre. The only way to describe it was like plankton, like from the sea, it was in the air. We saw it for a few seconds before it went."

Liz Cormell encountered plenty of activity in the bishop's room that she could not rationally explain:

> *"We were sitting there with a few other people on the bed. It was an old-fashioned bed, with a wooden headboard and floorboard. We asked for any spirits present to make themselves known by answering questions with knocks – one knock for yes, two for no. There were knocks to our question - it was proper hard, definite knocking on wood, and it sounded like knocking on the headboard.*
>
> *"We thought it could have been a member of the public doing it, so we got them all to stand away from the*

> bed. A camera was setup to record the bed, while me and Dave sat on the bed and held hands, to show that we weren't doing it.
>
> "We were still getting responses. It said that it saw us, that it lived there. We were getting lots of knocks for a 'yes' answer. It was exciting. Then I asked if it could do anything other than knock for yes.
>
> "Then –
>
> **"knockknockknockknockknockknock knockknockknockknockknockknock!**
>
> "It went mad knocking!
>
> "It couldn't have been the members of the public doing it. It wasn't Dave, I would have seen him or felt his body moving as he knocked.
>
> "I knew something was there. I couldn't get a handle on who it was, it's always difficult in the Ram Inn. I can't say who it was, whether it was a man or woman."

After the investigation had officially ended, most people left the buildings; but Liz, Dave and Paul Dyason decided to spend the night in the bishop's bedroom. There are three beds in this room, so it was a bed each.

"Liz couldn't get to sleep," Paul remarked, "as she's a medium and kept seeing people watching her."

"We were just waiting for something to happen," said Liz. "It was warm outside but absolutely freezing in the room. It was probably because of the stone walls. I was nervous, just waiting for something to happen. In the end I fell to sleep a little bit. Then something dropped on the bottom of the bed by my feet. I quickly looked over at Dave and Paul, and I saw they were asleep. It wasn't them. So I told whatever it was to go away."

This seemed to work, but whatever was in the bishop's bedroom was too curious to leave Liz alone for long: "Later something got in bed by me. Then it shoved me over. I said, "Fine, I'm leaving!" I spent the night in the car. There is a rumour of an incubus in the Ram Inn, though I don't exactly believe it."

The shattered glass

Simone Taylor's experience in the bishop's room was different but equally as shocking. She was with a small group; a couple of people were lying on the floor after finishing a bout of barrel tipping, and Simone was sitting on a bed:

> *"I had placed a glass cup on the top of the barrel when I suddenly felt a burst of anger. It was irrational! It was intense, venomous anger out of nowhere. There was no reason for it.*

I was looking at a person sitting opposite, and I wanted to kick his ass! I was totally enraged, and I felt like I could really hurt him. It was very alarming and I could not understand why I felt so angry.

"As I leaned forward the glass flew off the barrel towards the bloke.

"I don't have much recollection of it. The next thing I know, everyone is screaming and moving out the way after stating I had shouted at him something along the lines of [expletives] and apparently the glass then shot off the barrel with great force straight at him. It did not break but everyone was terrified. It scared us all! We were all freaked out, and the bloke was really scared.

"We had no idea how it flew off. There was no one close to knock it over. We tried jumping up and down, in case floorboards were jarring, but we couldn't knock over the glass again. I recall being sat on the edge of the middle bed in the bishop's room. I was not within reaching distance of the barrel that the group

had been using to try and get the glass to move on it.

"This borders on trance mediumship, as in a spirit channelling itself through a person – something I have great scepticism over 99% of the time, but I cannot explain this one away at all. It is like the seconds or however long it lasted have been totally erased from my memory. Could it have been a case of telekinesis? Possibly. I have heard encounters of projecting artefacts with the power of the mind. The most likely suggestion here would be trance. Now I think the bloke was the target as he was the one asking spirits to prove they were present.

"I just cannot explain the glass flying over, or why I was so angry. I know that afterwards I felt really drained."

Paul added a nugget of information on the words that Simone cannot remember saying. He was in the bishop's room when the incident took place, and believes that Simone was temporarily taken over, or possessed by some entity: "It spoke through her and said, "How's that for a parlour trick?" It wasn't a different voice that came out, but a different tone. Afterwards she didn't even know that she had said it."

Some of the hostile entities rumoured to inhabit the bishop's room are alleged to throw objects at visitors, especially if people sit down on a bed. As discussed by Simone, a theory could be that she was absorbing the emotions of the spirits, who then threw the glass; or they exploited her previously dormant telekinetic ability to throw the glass. There may not be spirits involved at all. It is all speculation. It remains that a glass flew across the bishop's room, and there is no satisfactory answer for it.

Transfigurations at the Ram Inn

That same evening Dave had a very similar incidence in the same bed in the bishop's room: he projected a growling sound from his mouth that he cannot explain or understand. Liz observed something of an animal in Dave, relating how after he was drawn to this middle bed in the bishop's room he turned to look at her and his features seemed to change – "he looked like a snarling dog."

This 'transfiguration' does not seem to have been an isolated incident. Rachel Penny felt herself being taken over by an entity during a séance at the Ram Inn:

> *"I opened myself up... I felt the energies. I felt myself tingling. Something was happening. Everyone saw me changing – my WOLF t-shirt was turning into a hooded top, my hair was getting long, and poking*

> *out, turning from my blonde to literally black.*
>
> *"I wasn't scared of what was happening, and I was aware of it all. A spirit was standing on the same space as me. It was female. Her features and energies were transforming me into her. Everyone was asking me questions. She wanted to speak through me, but I was not far enough gone to allow her to. My hands couldn't write anything, either, so I couldn't do automatic writing.*
>
> *"Then she left me. I was very drained afterwards."*

Scepticism

In spite of these reports of activity at the Ancient Ram Inn, there is mixed opinion on the supernatural quality of what happens there. An unnamed investigator is cautiously sceptical:

> *"It's supposed to be one of the most haunted places in the world, but nothing really happened to me. I picked up on a few things and that was about it. The Ram Inn is like a junkyard. The owner [John*

> *Humphries] wanders about when you're investigating, and I'm not sure if he sets things up. He has private quarters there, in which no one is allowed, and he might have routes from there to other parts of the Ram Inn, like they used to in old places. When we have heard footsteps it might just be him going around on unseen routes.*
>
> *"Once when we were going into a room, the door was shut and he said that when he opened it, they'd be plenty of orbs, so we should get our cameras ready. He banged on the door with a heavy staff, and then opened it. This could have dislodged dust on the inside, and created orbs. [Sceptics claim orbs are lens flare or dust, rather than spirit energies.]*

Another source questions the activity at the Ram Inn:

> *"The Ram Inn has had no reports of being haunted up until the present owner acquired the property. Whether Mr. Humphries is being haunted by poltergeist activity that is solely attracted to him, has a vivid imagination, or simply exploits the*

> *dereliction and age of the building for his gain is down to individual assumption."*

Others such as Paul Dyason are more enthusiastic:

> *"It's my favourite place. I am convinced it's very haunted, I'm certain. I'm not so sure about some of the stories about it, there's a certain amount of embellishment that goes on, like Chinese Whispers. But it doesn't mean there's no truth in it.*
>
> *"I don't know how John [Humphries] lives there! There was one occasion I could've stayed there for the night by myself, alone, as there was no one else there. I thought about it, and I went [home]! It's the only time I've done that. Liz advised me to stay only if I had a strong religious conviction."*

"It's one of the best places I've been to," Liz agreed. "I'd almost guarantee you that something would happen if you came with me. "

Conversation with a Murderer's Ghost

Interview with Simone Taylor

Derby Gaol is a museum in the remains of Derby's old Friar Gate Gaol. From 1756 to 1846, prisoners were kept in cells here, and it was the location for many hangings and beheadings. The buildings survived in some form or other until 1997, when it was bought by Richard Felix - a paranormal investigator, historian and a star of TV series, 'Most Haunted.' He restored two cells to something resembling their original state and opened up Derby Gaol as a museum and paranormal attraction. Among the supernatural encounters reported at Derby Gaol are Richard Felix's sighting of a grey haze in the shape of a person, gliding down a corridor; and heavy cell doors have closed by themselves.[26] It was visited by 'Most Haunted' in 2002.

Simone Taylor and members of the WOLF team have conducted a number of vigils in the cells at Derby Gaol. One visit in particular was quiet, with little luck in communicating with spirits. On other occasions, they have discovered orb activity in the cells; and there have been noticeable temperature changes and reports of people feeling uneasy.

---

[26] http://www.derbygaol.com

"About a week later I was using a Ouija board with my sister and mom," said Simone. "We made contact almost immediately, which is highly unusual. At first it was mixed messages but a very strong response – we could not make out the words so it was a process of elimination using yes/no questions, e.g. is it a spirit we have been in contact with recently, or it from a building one of us had visited recently? We did however keep getting the word 'sex' come up, which was a little bit concerning."

The Ouija board session was unexpectedly intense. There was information that no one knew the slightest thing about. They asked if this spirit had hurt someone, which received an affirmative answer; and then they got the name Batty, which did not mean anything to them.

From the information given through the Ouija board, they learned from this Batty person that he had committed sexual crimes against two children aged nine and ten that he later murdered. The year of the crimes was given. He had been an inmate of Derby Gaol before his execution, and had written a letter apologising for what he had done.

"All the way throughout the session the word "sorry" kept being spelt out," Simone continued. "Every time I asked what he was sorry about it spelt "sex." Thereafter the information just became repetitive and gradually dwindled away so that the planchette no longer moved. It was a strange experience and all of us commented how we could feel the atmosphere lift around us when the spirit was no longer present."

Unsure whether she had perhaps subconsciously picked up this information from her earlier trip, Simone returned to Derby Gaol. She wanted to eliminate the possibility that she had unwittingly affected the Ouija board session. There was nothing on the cells' walls or in the Gaol's history that matched the murderer's information. For Simone this was startling confirmation that the entity talking through the Ouija board was genuine.

A few weeks later, Simone and Vanessa Penny accompanied Richard Felix and his paranormal research group on a visit to Blackpool. On the spur of the moment, Simone approached Mr. Felix to discuss her information on the murderer and its links to Derby Gaol.

"He seemed interested when I told him about the Ouija board and what the person had told us," Simone said. "He was interested but more out of politeness. When I mentioned about the letter and the apology, Richard was really, really startled. He said, "How do you know about that? No one knows about that!"

"A sorry letter and other items had come along with Derby Gaol when he took it over, and it gave the same information that we picked up from the Ouija board. No one knew about the letter except Richard. There was no possible way either I or anyone else could know about it, as it was not in the public domain. He thought it was amazing. He was really enthusiastic, and really wanted to do something with it. He said he wanted to follow it up and indicated that this would make for a fantastic interview. But in the next week or so he left 'Most Haunted,' and couldn't do anything about what I had found out."

After crashing into a dead end with Richard Felix, Simone carried out research into the information given by the Ouija board. She discovered that a George Batty did in fact rape a girl, and this girl had the correct name as given in the session. Initially the records suggested that the girl was 16 when raped, but Simone found a document that gave the age as 10, matching the Ouija board information.

The author has attempted to make contact with Richard Felix on several occasions to get his reaction, but has been declined a reply.

Haunting at Minehead

Interview with Dawn Goding

Dawn Goding was living with her husband in a flat in Minehead, Somerset. It was in the High Street, a property in the old terraced style. After conversion from an attic, there had been open access into their flat from downstairs until Dawn determinedly put locks on the doors. This secured their property from intruders – and from an old man in particular, who lived downstairs and was in his seventies.

The atmosphere was heavy in the flat. Dawn could feel this weight upon her as she walked up the stairs to her home. At first, the strange activity was minor: objects were mysteriously moved and found in different rooms, and doors were opened even though they had shut them. They thought it could have been the old man from downstairs, but it continued after the doors were locked.

She was not left alone during her sleep:

> "It was winter, and I was in bed. Something woke me up. There was a figure stood over me, looking at me. I was still half-asleep. It might have been the bloke downstairs but afterwards we checked and the doors were all locked. It happened again another time. I woke up and this time I was more wide awake. I

saw the same figure at the bottom of the bed again, looking at me. I got a feeling that it was a man. It was dark and shadowy. We checked the locks [afterwards] and they were all fine.

"I never felt threatened. Even when I saw it, I never felt it was menacing or dangerous. I wasn't scared of it. But it was always like something was there in the flat."

Dawn described an incident in the kitchen: "I was cooking when I heard footsteps coming up the stairs. I heard someone walk in and sit at the table, so I started chatting to them, thinking it was my husband. When I turned around there was no one there – absolutely no one."

Caldicot Castle

Interview with Dawn Goding

True believers can be a strange lot: people sometimes so fanatical about the paranormal or influenced by clichés of the genre that they will do the most outlandish things.

Dawn Goding and her sister visited Caldicot Castle on a public investigation with an unnamed paranormal group. It was not WOLF. Caldicot Castle was a powerful stronghold in Monmouthshire throughout the medieval era, having originally been built by the Normans. After falling into ruin, its grandeur was restored in late Victorian times with conversion to a family residence.[27] It is located in the south-eastern corner of Wales, close to the border with England and opposite Bristol across the mouth of the River Severn.

Among the castle's reputed array of ghosts and spirits are hooded monks and shadowy figures, grey ladies and poltergeists. People have witnessed furniture moving by itself in the Gatehouse banqueting hall.

This was not enough for the intrepid paranormal investigators. Dawn could not hide her amusement at unorthodox attempts during the vigil to make contact with the castle's incorporeal inhabitants:

---

[27] http://www.caldicotcastle.co.uk

"The medium was using the whole group of people to get answers from the spirits as he asked the spirits questions aloud. We were all being asked to step forwards or backwards [moving if they felt they were pulled or pushed by spirits]*, to give a yes or no reply. It was like line dancing. One bloke was flipping and flopping all over the place; the medium was egging him on, telling the spirits to use the man to talk to us. Then the man fell down in a heap. The medium said, "This place is clean." The bloke who had flipped over recovered quickly and said, "Yes, she's gone, the spirit's gone through the door* [to the after-life]*."*

"Me and my sister started giggling and then laughing out loud because it was so stupid. This got us an evil look from the medium. A person asked if the place was empty of spirits now, as they had gone through 'the door.' The medium said that the spirit had gone through the door, but things can come <u>back</u> through doors. Not a very convincing reply.

"The bloke that was flopping was a fanatic. In one room there was a little

robin flying around; the bloke asked us if we could hear noises, but it was just this bird fluttering in there. He thought it was something else. He was comical in himself. Maybe he truly was having an experience – or just messing about."

The Pervy Poltergeist:
Haunting at a Tanning Salon

Interview with Dawn Goding

Sometimes WOLF ('World Oneiric Life Force') is asked to conduct private investigations by people who fear that their homes or businesses are afflicted by supernatural activity. On one occasion, the WOLF paranormal research team was called to a tanning salon where the owners were worried about a number of bizarre occurrences.

Dawn Goding and Liz Cormell travelled to the salon to meet the owner and to carry out a preliminary search of the premises. They were told how the next-door neighbour, who lived in his property, had complained to the salon's estate agent. He was angry about the loud bangs and noises during the night he heard coming from the tanning salon, which usually happened around 3am or 4am, a couple of times a week. He thought that squatters were in there and wanted them out. However, there were no squatters in the building, and, as far as the owner knew, the salon was empty during the night. The salon owner had no idea how the noise was happening.

A more shocking incident involved the owner's daughter. After being spray-tanned one evening, she was alone in the tanning room; her mother had left her to dry out, which involved her standing still, naked, with her arms spread out and her legs slightly apart. A few minutes later when the salon owner was returning, she saw her daughter come running out of the room in severe distress.

The daughter had been perfectly content standing in the room until she happened to glance at the tops of her arms. She saw that two handprints had been made in the spray-tan as it had dried. From the way the handprints were positioned, it looked like something had grabbed her arms from behind. It would have been impossible to do it to herself by accident or design because of how they were positioned, and they had not been there when the mother had left. The daughter had not felt it happen, nor observed any other person in the room. She only freaked out when she saw the handprints.

From talking to the salon owner, Dawn and Liz judged that she was levelheaded and not making the stories up. Her husband was cautiously sceptical, but said the handprints on his daughter's arms were extremely peculiar.

The preliminary search by Dawn and Liz proved more active than the full-blown investigation held by WOLF at a later date, when all they encountered was banging and tapping in one room.

The focus of much of the activity and energy was the tanning room. It had a large black tent in there, to protect against damage by the spray. Dawn described the atmosphere in there as feeling really heavy and claustrophobic. Liz used her gifts as a clairsentient to pick up on a man who felt the place belonged to him, and whose domain was the back of the shop.

Liz saw a figure move through the stairs. Research later showed that the stairs originally used to be the other way round in the property, and they had been moved to allow access upstairs. Therefore the space this figure moved into would have been some sort of room before; it would not have been stairs. Liz also saw a shadow walk out of the wall towards the door, towards the same place that the owner's daughter had her experience. An EMF meter was used, and while the readings just outside the door were empty, there was a sudden and unexplained EMF spike, which was very high and lasted for around 30 or 40 seconds.

The activity in the house was possibly linked to whatever was there before the tanning salon. Dawn theorised a link between the house, which was built around 1901-05, and coalminers, as there used to be a brickworks and coalmine opposite the building.

Since the full private investigation the salon has become quieter. The paranormal activity has slackened. The worst of the weird seems to be the hanging decorations on door handles starting to swing all by themselves.

Middleton Hall

Interview with Dawn Goding

It can be sickening when a person's faith is damaged by a 'false prophet.' Even the most amazing apparition will be regarded with suspicion, as Dawn Goding discovered during a paranormal investigation in North Warwickshire.

Middleton Hall is a grand old building. It is situated close to Tamworth, and the initial phases of its construction date back to the late 13th century. Middleton's Great Hall was erected in the Tudor era - Queen Elizabeth I spent two nights here in 1575 - and a Georgian west wing dates from the late 18th century; but for much of the 20th century it was allowed to fall into disrepair. After recent restoration Middleton Hall is now a Grade II listed building, used for weddings and conferences. Among its features are 40 acres of gardens and woodland, the largest man-made lake in Warwickshire, a theatre, and a Tudor barn complex converted into craft shops.

There have been reports of ghosts and poltergeist activity at Middleton Hall, including a 17th century Civil War-era gentleman and a Victorian lady wearing a scarlet dress.

Dawn and her husband arrived for an investigation at Middleton Hall organised by an unnamed paranormal group. It was not WOLF. While waiting for the start, they observed a woman reading a history of Middleton Hall, and later were surprised to find out that she was the medium - the individual with special skills and awareness that allows them sensitivity to spirits. Dawn was unimpressed by this effort to learn more about Middleton Hall's background, which undermined the medium's authenticity.

"People say that you can read up on a place to get information before an investigation," she said, "but I don't do it. That way, if I pick up on something I can't say I've cheated, or picked it up sub-consciously and given a description that's not right."

Things got worse. During the investigation, the medium began describing a spiritual presence she felt in a room. As Dawn looked to a space opposite the medium, she could see on the wall an information plate that contained a picture and details which were exactly like the supposed spirit.

Dawn was scathing: "How can you trust she was telling the truth about things, or if not purposely, then even sub-consciously using this information? "She's a fraud," my husband said. I was not impressed by this lady; I couldn't believe a word she said."

The medium was patronising towards a member of the public: a young man in his early twenties. She told him he had 'the gift,' after benevolently listening to his tales of seeing spirits and ghosts throughout his childhood, and his parents telling him he was mad and just had imaginary friends. This ability to 'see things' had persisted into adulthood, and he was at the investigation at Middleton Hall to prove himself.

Whatever confidence the young man possessed was later squashed by the medium. When the investigation moved into the nursery at the old hall, he seemed to sense a woman who was dressed well and seemed 'nice.' "The medium said he was wrong," Dawn related. "She was saying, "Oh no, no, no, I've got a man, and he's malevolent, he's forcing his way in." I know that everyone interprets things differently but she cut off the young man. He was put off from saying anything else; he shut up the rest of the night."

The investigation at Middleton Hall did throw up a number of uncanny occurrences that deepened Dawn's regret that the full potential of the place had not been unlocked.

Her husband saw an apparition, but steadfastly refused to accept it was genuinely supernatural:

> *"We were doing a glass thing [divination] in the main hall, and my husband was sitting opposite me. He saw something at the back of the hall – he said it was a man; it looked like an old-fashioned headteacher, in 1950s stuff, with receding hair, grey, bushy at the sides maybe. This person had on a long black coat, with some sort of white cravat thing tied around the throat but sort-of trailing down the*

> *chest. It was sitting down on one of the seats at the back of the hall but then got up and walked out of the door.*
>
> *"I turned around to see what my husband was looking at and I saw the door shutting, but I didn't see the man. Two or three others saw the door shutting. We thought it could have been a draught. The host went and looked, but there was no one there. My husband thought it could have been someone who worked there but there was no one else in the building."*

They were on a walkabout in Middleton Hall and entered a room that seemed split between being an office and a toy room. The medium called to spirits, asking them to show themselves by causing a rocking horse to move. Most people were looking at this rocking horse. Dawn and her husband were aware of something else happening: "We heard the noise first, and then saw it as we turned. We were looking at an old-time spinning top that had started moving across an old-fashioned sideboard. It seemed to start spinning from an angle. There was no one near it. It was spinning, then it hit a few toys and stopped. It wasn't just me and my husband that saw it, a group of three or four women saw it too."

The Hellfire Caves

Interview with Paul Dyason

Background

The Hell-Fire Caves are situated in the village of West Wycombe, Buckinghamshire.[28] They are sometimes called the West Wycombe Caves. In the years around 1748-52 an existing chalk-mine was given a deep extension of tunnels, and the resultant works were was considered marvels of the age for their feats of engineering.

The tunnels twist deep into the earth for half a mile. The passageways are slightly inclined downwards, so that the descent is not always obvious to visitors. From the entrance they progress for a short distance before taking a sharp left turn. The tunnels regularly branch-off and meet-up again, thereby creating shapes such as triangles and crossed circles. There are numerous alcoves in the tunnel walls. The path takes in large man-made caverns such as the banqueting hall, before finally crossing a river nicknamed the River Styx (in Greek myth this was the river that flowed through hell) beyond which lies the 'Inner Temple.' Here the tunnels end, around 300 feet below the surface. Directly above the spot is a church containing the Dashwood family mausoleum.

---

[28] Please refer to the official website: http://www.hellfirecaves.co.uk

This extensive system of tunnels and caves was creation of Sir Francis Dashwood, a local aristocrat and founder of the Hellfire Club that met between 1749 and 1760. This was a club for noblemen, politicians and other influential 'persons of quality.' The Hellfire Caves were constructed specifically to host their notorious gatherings: rumours hinted at orgies and debaucheries, where prostitutes were dressed as nuns and used for entertainment; and there were accusations of pagan rituals, black masses, even the worship of Satan.

The Hellfire Club is also associated with Aleister Crowley (1875-1947), an infamous occultist and magician who used the Club's motto – "Fais ce que tu voudras", or "Do what thou wilt," as a philosophy of life. Crowley alleged he was in contact with astral entities from a different, higher dimension - creatures described by other people as 'demons' or 'elementals.'

There are many supernatural tales associated with the caves, notably the apparition of Paul Whitehead, an influential member of the Hellfire Club, and the ghost of the 'White Lady,' who haunts the passageways.

Investigation

Paul Dyason attended a public investigation of the Hellfire Caves organised by Ghostfinder Paranormal Society (GPS). This was a couple of days prior to GPS's involvement with Living TV's live Halloween 2010 event, similarly held at the Caves. Paul referred to their preference for a scientific approach to paranormal investigation, using devices such as EMF meters (electromagnetic field) and EVP recorders (electronic voice phenomena) and placing less emphasis on divination, Ouija boards and other psychic tools of the trade.

Fifty people were at the investigation, a larger than usual number of people. GPS began with a short talk that explained their organisation's approach, presenting EVP and photographic evidence. The public was split into three smaller, more manageable groups.

There was a vigil in the Inner Temple. This is a place where the Hellfire Club is alleged to have conducted black magic and orgies. Paul was disappointed with the results of his EVP recordings. The GPS staff member leading this group was more successful, and recorded EVP material that seemed to suggest a muffled voice. [On inspection by the author, this EVP might have been caused by winds blowing through the tunnels and creating a moaning effect.]

Another vigil was held in a section of the caves reputedly haunted by Paul Whitehead, the member of the Hellfire Club mentioned above. The group called out to any spirits that were nearby, asking them to show themselves by, for instance, tapping an object. They had been standing there for several minutes when Paul felt something touch his left shin. He felt the material of his jeans actually being pushed before his skin was touched. Some time later Paul was standing against a wall in this area. There were electric candles on this wall. He was surprised when they began flickering very animatedly.

There was no straightforward explanation, as the electrics were working without fault elsewhere in the caves.

"We asked for the lights to flicker more," said Paul, "and they did, one light went mad and it almost went out. This happened for five minutes or so."

GPS said it was a quiet night by the location's usual standards. The atmosphere in the Hellfire Caves did not feel eerie to Paul: perhaps because he is familiar with the location, having visited many times before, and the greater number of people made it difficult to identify any unexplained activity.

Ghosts of Edinburgh

Interview with Paul Dyason

One of the most famous haunted locations in Scotland is the Edinburgh Vaults. It has served as the location for many paranormal investigations filmed for television, such as 'Most Haunted.'

The Edinburgh Vaults consist of more than a hundred chambers formed in the arches of the South Bridge in Edinburgh, Scotland. The bridge was constructed in 1788, and for several decades this was the vicinity of one of Edinburgh's worst slums. It housed the city's poor, and living conditions were utterly appalling. It was a notorious red-light district, filled with brothels and pubs, where criminal activity was rampant: the murderous body snatchers, Burke and Hare, hunted for prey in this inhospitable district. The Vaults were abandoned in the 1830s, and filled in with rubble some time in the mid-19th century before their rediscovery in the late 20th century.

The WOLF staff members that travelled to Edinburgh were Paul Dyason, David Ball and Liz Cormell. They visited all three of the locations used on the Halloween 2006 'Most Haunted Live' shows – namely Blair Street Vaults, Niddry Street Vaults and Mary King's Close.

They could only visit the Blair Street section of the Vaults on a night-time public tour. Keeping to the back of the group, they felt that there was something out of the ordinary here, but they could not use their usual electronic equipment and divination techniques. They could hear pebbles pinging behind them as they moved through the chambers.

Paul happened to look back and was startled to see something shadowy beginning to form. It became more visible. "It was the figure of a young woman," said Paul. "At first I could see the right hip and thigh materialising, then the rest of the body formed. It was wearing a long white dress. I asked Liz if she could see it; she said, "Yes, I can see the lady there." We shone a torch at it which caused us to lose our night vision."

They could not see the apparition after recovering from their disorientation. It had gone.

"I didn't go there expecting it to happen," Paul continued. "Liz also saw it, so it wasn't a hallucination – it was actually there, it wasn't seen psychically. I was stunned more than anything else. It didn't feel nasty. At no point was I frightened. Liz picked up on the active spirits; she said they were pleased at the work of the people doing the re-enactments and telling stories about the place so well. They were benevolent."

The Vaults at Niddry Street have a reputation for aggressive poltergeist activity: people have allegedly been attacked, their injuries ranging from cuts and bruises to a broken wrist. Paul, Liz and David were here at Niddry Street alone for an investigation until 5am. It seems to have been a quiet night. There is a disused stone circle that was purportedly used for pagan worship, or witchcraft; it is supposed to contain a demon. Paul and David stood in this circle, despite Liz's warnings. Afterwards David told the others that a superficial scratch had appeared on his arm which had almost cut through the skin. He was not entirely sure how it had happened.

Mary King's Close is a tourist attraction in the Old Town area of Edinburgh, near the Royal Mile. It is a collection of old streets and houses, some seven stories high, that were submerged as the development of the city in the 19th century accelerated and Edinburgh expanded upwards rather outwards, filling in hills and covering what lay beneath. Buildings were constructed on top of each other, sometimes literally leaving the older buildings underground.

"They're supposed to be haunted," said Paul. "They're certainly a curious place. It's surreal: you can go beneath the street level. There were vagabonds and prostitutes down there, even the plague some time ago. But I didn't pick up on anything [supernatural]."

Theatre on the Steps

Interviews with Paul Dyason and Dawn Goding

Investigation

It was Halloween. WOLF was conducting a vigil at Theatre on the Steps, in Bridgnorth, Shropshire. It had been a quiet night, and the team was impatient to find paranormal activity in this haunted hot spot.

During a séance utilising glass divination in one of the upper rooms, Rachel Penny had suddenly felt poorly. Liz Cormell sensed the spirit of a German trying to communicate, which was a surprise to everyone. Later, Kevin Berrill became emotional, perhaps upset by private thoughts or sensations. After speaking to Liz he felt able to continue.

At the vigil were Rachel, Liz and Kevin, along with Dawn Goding, David Ball, Simone Taylor, Vanessa Penny and Paul Dyason.

They discovered a coffin lying among the theatre props. It looked and felt authentic, and to spark the atmosphere David volunteered to lie in the coffin with the lid placed down. The lid was heavy and took several people to lift. David was fully encapsulated by the coffin, as if he were dead.

"We had a divination session using the coffin lid," said Paul. "It was like table tipping, asking for the lid to be moved. We had our fingertips just touching the edge of the lid. We were calling out. Liz picked up upon a Reverend or vicar who was not happy with what we were doing. She got an angry vibe. He was causing the lid to move. It was shuffling a centimetre at a time. It was gradual. At the beginning the lid was on the coffin properly; at the end it had shifted so we could just peek in."

Dawn observed the same phenomenon. "We definitely saw the lid moving," she agreed. "It was moving up and to the side. We had our hands on top and we could feel it moving, not just see it. The first movement was most significant, it went a few centimetres; then softer movements, then a few big ones and then softer tapping. We asked Dave what was happening but he couldn't hear what we were saying."

David has film footage recorded from inside the coffin that seems to show that he passes out for a few seconds. There is also footage that allegedly shows the coffin lid moving, proving that no participant was cheating by physically moving it.

This lasted for around twenty to thirty minutes, until it ceased and David left the coffin.

Background

'Theatre on the Steps' is an actual theatre. It was established in 1962, using the skeleton of a church built in 1829 but actually on the site of an older chapel, founded around 1709.[29] The members of this church were not popular in Bridgnorth for much of the 18th century, ostensibly because the church's location was unfavourable, located on the Stoneway Steps and set into a steep hill that has caves beneath.

Among the supernatural phenomenon reported at Theatre on the Steps are apparitions, disembodied voices, and strange, unexplained smells.

Some of the WOLF staff that were present at the vigil were unaware of the location's history as a church. Paul said that it had a church-like atmosphere, but he did not know that it was originally a house of God. They seemed to believe that the coffin was only a stage prop. This might not necessarily be true: much of the furniture and furnishings at Theatre on the Steps were recycled from other locations in the West Midlands. Purchases in the 1960s included theatre curtains, switchboard and stage lighting from the demolished Midland Institute in Birmingham city centre; and theatre seats came from the long-gone Odeon Cinema in Coseley, near Dudley.

It is possible that the 'stage' coffin had some practical use in the past – obviously not for a burial, but for some purpose that imbued it with unusual properties.

---

[29] For a short history of Theatre on the Steps see the official website: http://www.theatreonthesteps.co.uk

The Dixie Dude Ranch

Interview with Simone Taylor

Simone Taylor and her boyfriend Lee were travelling in the United States of America on holiday. They stopped in Texas, initially staying close to the Alamo - site of the famous battle of 1836 in which famous Texans such as Davy Crockett and Jim Bowie fought to the death against Mexican troops in a bloody battle for Texan independence. There was also a 'haunted hotel' in San Antonio, Texas, that proved disappointing to the fearless ghost-hunter.

Simone hoped to find something out-of-the-ordinary, some spiritual energy; but she found nothing at the Alamo, and in San Antonio little more than a bathroom door that swung by itself. Simone decided to stop looking for anything mysterious or unusual, and chose instead to enjoy the holiday.

They moved on to the Dixie Dude Ranch in Bandera, not far from San Antonio. It is a working ranch, founded in 1901, with longhorn cattle, goats and pigs kept, and home to cowboys preparing for rodeos. There are cabins and horse riding for tourists. The landscape is straight out of a Wild West film, the arid Texas hill country gouged with valleys, and pocked with cactus, yucca and Texas Live Oak.

One night in their cabin, Simone woke from sleep. She opened her eyes to see a tall, shadowy figure standing over her, not far from her face, and looking directly at her. At first thinking it was her boyfriend, she soon changed her mind when she felt Lee next to her in bed.

"I could see the silhouette of the thing," said Simone.

> *"It was huge, its head was elongated and I couldn't see a neckline. I thought maybe it had long hair. It was bulky and there were shapes around the middle, like it had a belt on or equipment. It was definitely a bloke! Instantly I thought of a Native American Indian and that image stuck with me.*
>
> *"Looking at the silhouette was like watching static: the image was prickly, not entirely clear. I can only describe it as 'pins and needles,' like what you get in your hands and feet. That's what it looked like.*
>
> *"It seemed curious about me, standing completely over me as I was in bed. When it knew I was awake and aware of it, it started backing away. It took a step away, towards the bottom of the bed, only it didn't seem to be a walking movement, it was very smooth and more like gliding. As I blinked it just went, it disappeared - it faded into nothing.*

> "I was watching it for what seemed like ages, but it was probably only a couple of seconds. I hadn't been scared. To think now that a figure or person was standing over me in the black of the night is terrifying, but at the time, there was such a feeling of calmness and no panic at all. It's very difficult to explain.
>
> "I took photos of the room the next day. Where it had been standing over the bed there was a bright light, an orb."

The next day, Simone and Lee went riding with the Dixie Dude ranch-hands, and she took a chance to ask if there had ever been any ghostly occurrences reported at Dixie Dude. She did not reveal which room they were staying in, briefly describing what happened the previous night. The cowboys were excited and straight away asked Simone if she was staying in the Jingles cabin – out of all the twenty or so cabins at Dixie Dude they were able to identify the right one.

"They didn't know which one I was staying in," said Simone, "but they guessed right. They said I was staying in their most active cabin. They asked me if the taps had been running water without being turned on. This had happened before, and the plumbers they called in couldn't find any problems. They said that an American Indian was there at Dixie Dude; he had been seen around the campfire, and seen on the grounds of the ranch trying to light a fire; he'd also been seen in the kitchens.

"They said that he appeared in the shower in Jingles cabin whenever a woman was in there. They might have been joking about that, though." Simone did not seem entirely convinced.

She wrote to the ranch afterwards about what she experienced but they did not want to know. The possibility of paranormal activity did not correspond with the public image of Dixie Dude ranch they were trying to project.

"It was an amazing surprise for what was a previously unknown location for suspected hauntings," she said. "It's rare to see a full apparition but there was no doubt about what I saw that night, later verified by employees at the ranch. This particular cabin definitely warrants further investigation - just a shame Texas is so many miles away! I will return!"

The Haunted Church

Personal account of a WOLF paranormal investigation

The investigation took place at a Black Country church with medieval origins. Its long, troubled history and reports of supernatural activity attracted the attention of the WOLF group, who decided that this atmospheric building was ripe for exploration. I was lucky enough to accompany the core members of the WOLF team and a select number of associate members.

The darkening nights and higher levels of electromagnetic activity in the local weather systems at that time offered the prospect of an eventful evening.

On passing the threshold there was the expected musty smell, though strongly-tinged with incense. Inside it was quiet and gloomy. Candles were sprinkled across the stalls and statues, the flickering lights creating shadows that seemed to shift.

"I tasted blood in my mouth"

On the initial tour of the site we were shown the vestry. This used to be part of the ancient churchyard. I did not feel anything unusual, and it seemed quite ordinary. However, some members of the group with psychic sensitivity reported feeling very strange while in the room; one person said they felt like they were interrupting a meeting, perhaps of some secret society; another person tasted blood in their mouth.

From an appraisal of the vestry I could see WOLF's high professional standards in action: placed on a table were two old-fashioned coins acting as trigger objects, which it was hoped mischievous spirits would move; a Dictaphone was left recording; and an infra-red camera was on open display recording the room and doorway for activity, but with another camera also recording from a secret location in the room, to prevent deceptions. There was no way anyone could cheat.

Later when we moved past the stalls by the altar, I was aware of a low, strange sound, like many whispering voices. Maybe it was the heavy atmosphere getting to me, or an echo – there were many echoes in this church. I didn't hear it again.

"The motion detector was going crazy"

The investigators split into three teams. I was with Gemma Taylor and Vanessa Penny. We completed base readings. It was around 10:35pm.

We began exploring the stalls. Motion detection equipment had been set-up on a particular stall, and Gemma checked that it was working correctly. We moved down the aisle. I was at the back, looking at the dark panorama and at a statue of the Virgin Mary, surrounded by candles.

Suddenly there was an explosion of noise behind us. Everyone jumped. The motion detector was going crazy. Things had been quiet, and that peacefulness was shattered. We could see nothing behind us that might have set off the detector. There was no rational explanation, other than it had been set-off by the earlier test.

We moved down the aisle and sat in the corner by a smaller altar. It was dark but not too cold. Gemma and Vanessa started calling out to any spirits that were present, asking them to show themselves.

They tried pendulum dowsing. This involved holding a pendulum and calling out to spirits, asking them to move the pendulum in response to questions; if they wanted the spirits to spell something out, they called out letters of the alphabet until the pendulum's violent motion confirmed this was the correct one; and this continued until a word had been spelt out.

They discovered the identity of a spirit called Henry, who seemed to communicate that he was a 'reverend' from the 1730s, and was now protecting people in the church – including us.

I later learned that the other teams had made contact with other vicars using this same kind of dowsing. This was not unexpected – we were in a church after all – though I believe that non-clerical entities also made themselves known.

We took turns at sitting in a chair near this corner. The church guide later told us that the chair dated from the 16th century, that it had belonged to one of the first vicars of the church and had been associated with previous paranormal activity. I admit that I felt more comfortable in the chair than sitting on the floor, and I was reminded of a teacher sitting at a school assembly as I looked across the stalls. I cannot say that I felt very different sitting there, or sensed anything unusual, which is what I think was expected of me. I wondered if I was being tested for susceptibility to suggestion.

The candles were now going out one by one, and the gloom was growing.

"We heard footsteps racing ahead of us…"

There were odd reports from the vicinity of a pulpit: Vanessa had a sense of marching soldiers and a tall man; while Gemma began to feel strange and uneasy after standing there. A hymn book from the pulpit was also scanned with an EMF meter and gave unusually high readings. What made it more peculiar was a photograph that Simone Taylor had taken of a large light anomaly – an 'orb' – which she could not explain. It seemed to be hovering over the pulpit at exactly the place where Gemma had stood.

Our group investigated another part of the church which was disused and seemed physically dangerous, with debris and layers of dust. It was much darker due to lack of illumination, so we relied on torches.

Even as we approached the area, Gemma and I thought we heard footsteps racing ahead of us. It could have been echoes of our own footsteps or those of other groups. I am not sure. Anyone who has been in this kind of environment will understand how little things can be exaggerated by the darkness and silence (which can lead to sensory deprivation) and by the effects of tiredness.

I saw things from the corner of my eye that almost startled me. After straining my eyes to focus on what seemed a strange white blob of a head at some fair distance from me, I reasoned that it was only a white book on an altar, which later I confirmed.

When a motion detector across from us went off twice, I queried what was happening. It was in this direction that Gemma thought she saw red dots through the murk, but in hindsight it could have been from the motion detector's battery indicator, rather than anything supernatural. On the occasions that it went off, there was nobody there. The church guide suggested it was "kids" playing, and I don't think he meant anything living.

"A focal point for some unknown entity…"

We returned to our original site for investigation - the stalls where the motion detector had earlier come alive to noisy effect. The other WOLF investigators were busy. There was pendulum dowsing, which seemed to be located on the same spot as the motion detector. People seemed to sense that these stalls were a focal point for some unknown entity.

I heard reference to a nearby stained glass window, which supposedly contained freemasonry or pagan symbols – and I noticed that the far-off statue of the Virgin Mary cast a shadow on the wall in this same spot.

Later on, I attempted to find a trigger object (in this case a toy tiger) using dowsing rods. This is a typical investigative technique: everyone has heard of dowsing for water, though probably not for tigers. This was a new experience for me. I searched along the stalls, feeling an occasional little tug of the dowsing rods (perhaps they were just heavy?) but I had absolutely no luck. Almost everyone else managed to find the tiger. My confidence was not significantly damaged.

The night was getting very late, and the investigation began to wind down. The atmosphere had gone flat. Little wonder, as people were tired. I listened to a little of what other people had experienced: one woman had heard something on the stairs shout, "Get out!", and others had heard high-pitched noises, some sort of vibrations that left them with heavy heads.

Perhaps I did not feel entirely convinced that any paranormal power was at work – it would probably have taken a full-blown manifestation to persuade me otherwise, which is asking a lot. I cannot fight my sceptical nature, though I am willing to contemplate the possibility of ghosts and the supernatural. I just need overwhelming, first-hand proof.

In any case, I went away from this Black Country church feeling that my imagination would be richer for the experience; and that cannot be a bad thing.

World Oneiric Life Force:
An overview
Article written in 2008

Ghouls and evil spirits beware – you may soon find yourselves hunted down by an eager team of paranormal investigators.

WOLF (which stands for 'World Oneiric Life Force,') is the name of a West Midlands-based group that is making its mark in the realms of supernatural research and advice. Not only are they actively exploring the country's most infamous haunted places: they are ghost hunters-for-hire, investigating strange occurrences in people's homes and businesses.

It was established in January 2007 by David Ball and Simone Taylor, who work alongside core team members Vanessa Penny and Gemma Woolridge. [Gemma Woolridge has since left the team, with Rachel Penny, Paul Dyason and Liz Cormell incoming as new members of staff. Associate members include Dawn Goding, Julie Bennett, Kevin Berrill and Gemma Taylor.]

Despite its short history the group has already become an item at psychic fayres, associating with the likes of Richard Felix of 'Most Haunted' fame in public vigils at Dudley Castle, Berkeley Castle in Gloucester and the infamous 'Galleries of Justice' in Nottingham.

They are all normal, young people with day-jobs and busy private lives, who share a zeal for the supernatural. Simone and Vanessa have been friends for years, attending local fright nights together. They met David through membership of a paranormal society; and after growing disillusioned with its clique-mentality and lack of professionalism they decided to form their own group – thus WOLF was born.

Their internet website contains extensive information on research into ghostly phenomenon, along with news of investigations and a forum for discussion. Interested members of the public are encouraged to join WOLF, and can gain core, associate and 'cub' membership of the group.

"I screamed like a girl!"

Gemma Woolridge was eager to explore her lifelong interest in the supernatural from the front-line after learning of WOLF's website from a work colleague. "I went on there and it looked like everything that I had ever wanted to be involved in, the mix of the paranormal and the spiritual healing," she said.

> *"I had been interested in it for a few years. I always felt that there was more out there than what the Catholic religion had taught me; there was more than heaven, hell and purgatory!*

> "When I was a child there were little coincidences in our house, such as hearing creaking on the stairs and lights flickering for no reason; I know this isn't necessarily paranormal, but after we left, my Dad told me that he had once seen a full manifestation travel through the living room wall.
>
> "When WOLF had a position come up for the role of research assistant I thought that it was an ideal opportunity to get involved more hands-on. So I applied - as you do - and when I met the others it was like we were old friends, I felt so comfortable just talking to them and the friendship has grown loads ever since.
>
> "We all work really hard to make WOLF what it should be. To me, being involved in WOLF isn't just a hobby, I've achieved so much and grown loads spiritually, emotionally, and I feel that together we can take on anything. Sorry if that sounds cheesy!"

David Ball was drawn to the mystical world after a lifelong sensitivity to all things psychic. He spent some time working on a church board that attempted to provide spiritual protection to a small village community where rumours of occultism and black magic were rife.

"I've always had a passion for the supernatural," he said, and revealed details of his first experience with a ghost: "I was in my bed and heard a click in the room, and turned to see a woman standing next to me. I couldn't believe it. It was like thick cigarette smoke, tangible and almost solid. I screamed like a girl, and it disappeared as my brother came rushing in."

"There was a green fuzzy energy right in front of me!"

WOLF has been actively delving into local mysteries. One of their favourites is the legend of 'Bella in the Wych Elm,' with its links to witchcraft, pagan sacrifice and murder.

In 1943 the rotted corpse of a woman was found stuffed in the hollow trunk of a witch-hazel tree at a lonely spot in Hagley Woods, near Stourbridge. The victim was never identified and gained the nickname 'Bella.' Her murder was never solved.

Many believe that the woman had been sacrificed by Satanists in some macabre ritual, as a police search of the undergrowth uncovered her severed hand. Occult tradition asserts that the spirit of a dead witch can be prevented from causing harm by being imprisoned in the hollow of a tree, and that a hand cut from a witch's corpse contains powerful magic. Perhaps this was the reason for 'Bella's' murder.

Simone has been researching the story for years, and has led on efforts to develop an understanding of the story by interviewing persons involved in the body's discovery and the police investigation. The WOLF team has also conducted vigils on the lane beside the woods where Bella's body was found.

Another of WOLF's stomping grounds is Dudley Castle, in the West Midlands. It is a location famous for its long history and the romantic appeal of the castle ruins set upon a hill – and as a place where unearthly spirits freely roam. In recent times it has gained popularity for its public ghost walks and late-night vigils watching for spooky activity.

WOLF scored notable successes after eventful nights in different parts of the castle ruins, as Gemma spectacularly confirmed when she spoke of her experiences:

> *"In part of the castle I saw a visual of a green fuzzy energy right in front of me! This was amazing especially when I saw that the energy moved! We learned that this was a butler who had died in the chamber.*
>
> *"My scariest experience was in the undercroft. During a group séance a monk was apparently standing behind me, and I felt a burning heat spread across my shoulders. According to the medium the monk was chanting in Latin and the word 'striven' appeared,*

and I was being poked with a red-hot poker!

"The medium said that this was because I had some sins that I need to confess to myself - these have yet to become known to me! But I was incredibly scared and I don't scare that easily."

Pubs and poltergeists

WOLF have organised a large number of overnight paranormal experiences, where members of the public can become investigators for the night. All sorts of high-tech gadgetry are used, such as the EMF meters seen in programmes like 'Most Haunted.'

At the behest of the proprietor of 'The Starving Rascal' pub at Brettell Lane, Brierley Hill, a private investigation was turned into a semi-public experience. Joining up with pub-goers, they held pendulum vigils and a séance in the reputedly-haunted cellar, finishing with a big Ouija session. "People went away buzzing," said Simone, "and everyone had a really good time."

The WOLF team has also answered many requests for their expertise and advice in investigating reports of mysterious phenomenon in private residences. WOLF show utter discretion and are careful to maintain confidentiality in sensitive cases.

A particularly creepy episode involved an alleged poltergeist at a Coventry property, after WOLF was contacted by distraught tenants panicked by the ghostly incidents that tormented their home. There were terrifying reports of screaming and cursing in empty rooms; arguments on staircases where no one had been standing; and things were so bad that one person had actually moved out and returned only when it had quietened down.

"They knew of WOLF through friends," said David, "and this sort of thing was unusual for them, out of character and highly unlikely to be a lie."

WOLF's vigils did not seem to catch any activity, but the two divination methods they used – pendulum dowsing and Ouija board – hinted at what could be causing the trouble. "We encountered a woman aged between fifty and sixty who was unhappy with the way she died," said David, "and she wanted it resolved before she could leave."

The phenomena recommenced after the WOLF team left, and became so horrifyingly intense that it finally drove out the occupiers. "There was a phone call one Friday, they were frantic - it had not gone away," said David. "They had wanted to leave for a while, and they couldn't stand any more – they left the house, abandoned it, and we haven't heard back since. The house is empty now, which is better for investigations, and we're trying to contact the landlord."

"There was something hateful and evil surrounding us"

Not all investigations have positive outcomes, nor are they pleasant experiences. This was proved emphatically by a frightening night the WOLF team spent at Temple Balsall, near Solihull.

WOLF held an overnight vigil at a medieval hall ascribed to the Knights Templar. They were a military-religious order from the Middle Ages which gained power and wealth from its role in the Crusades. Rumours circulated that they had discovered the Ark of the Covenant and the Holy Grail in the Holy Land. In 1307 the order was accused of witchcraft; their most prominent members were arrested, tortured into confessions and burnt at the stake.

The Knights Templar built a great hall and chapel sometime between 1160 and 1180 on a small hill at Temple Balsall, surrounded by wooded meadows close to the heart of the old Forest of Arden. External brickwork was added during the 18th century. Its glory days have long since passed, but it still retains an eldritch magic.

Little wonder that the WOLF team encountered a highly-charged atmosphere during their vigil at the hall – as it also happened to be Friday the 13^{th,} and was close to the 700th anniversary of the fall of the Knights Templar. By the end of the night everyone had come away drained of energy, feeling unnerved and reluctant to ever re-enter the old hall.

They brought their usual array of specialised equipment and techniques; typically the WOLF team are prepared with Dictaphones (to record sound), laser thermometers (which send red lights flying through the air, for sensing the temperature at the spot at which they are pointed,) night vision cameras, EMF meters (for probing changes in the electro-magnetic field, allegedly caused by paranormal activity,) besides tools such as Ouija boards.

There were no overtly disturbing or unusual incidents during the night; it was more of an overpowering sense of menace and foreboding that shook their senses. "Temple Balsall was great, but a little scary," said Gemma Woolridge. "You know when you just get a really bad feeling that something is going to happen?"

The team decided that they could endure no more and made a retreat. David and Simone were the last to leave. In their final few moments the pair suddenly felt anxious and heavy-headed, which was followed by an unwarranted flood of anger. "It was scary knowing that there was something hateful and evil surrounding us, a presence that wanted us out," said Simone. "I've never felt anything so strong."

As they finally left the Templar hall and began walking down a nearby lane, the rest of the group saw them and speculated upon the identity of the person that was seen momentarily walking alongside them. But there had only ever been the two of them. It was either a trick of the light, or something more sinister. Something was escorting them off the premises.

They hurriedly got into their car. David and Simone felt spaced-out and sick, with a sensation of being surrounded by something outside the car that was trying to force them away.

It was a psychic attack, and David suffered its effects for weeks with depression and lethargy, and other team members were similarly affected.

The shrieking thing at the séance

After hearing these spine-chilling tales, I needed to see the WOLF team in action, in hope of perhaps seeing real paranormal activity, to convince me of its authenticity – and to scare the living hell out of myself!

I joined an investigation of supposedly haunted woods at an unspecified location. Needless to say its history was steeped in wild gossip, and the darkness was deep enough for anything to be possible. The ground was strewn with old, rotting stumps, and a pervasive sense of decay hung over it all. Night fell quickly and the woods were soon pitch-black, punctuated by the intermittent flash of a camera. It made me feel even more disorientated.

We tried using a Ouija board to make contact with spirits. I could not help but remember the warnings issued by psychics, telling us that the things which communicate through Ouija boards are not always helpful little spirits, but sometimes entities with a malicious, even malevolent sense of humour.

"With these sessions you need to take things with a pinch of salt," said Simone. "There are things playing with you, and you've got to be careful. It's important to use tools like Ouija boards under strict control. Whatever you're communicating with could be mischievous or worse, calling you names, swearing, feeding on your worst fears and calling out things that it knows will hurt you. It's not a good thing to ask questions like "When will I die?" as you'll only get a bad answer."

I was surprised by the results of my first experience using a Ouija board. My finger was gently touching the planchette as I watched it move ever so slowly on its own volition, answering the questions put forth. It moved quicker and spelt out our names, one by one. This was unsettling, especially as I was fairly sure – but not certain - that nobody was cheating or deliberately moving the planchette. We each took turns to remove our finger and yet I saw it continue its motion across the board.

Towards midnight we began a séance, a flickering lantern and candles breaking the profound darkness. We gathered in a circle and held hands, applying 'psychic protection' to ourselves by a series of relaxation exercises. David called out to any spirits or entities that were present, asking them to make themselves known;

there was nothing at first, nothing more than little gnats irritating the back of my neck.

I could feel a very slight, cool breeze blowing through the trees to the right of me, and it was probably only coincidental that Simone was also looking in that direction, soon deciding to leave the circle in order to take readings. Later she told us that she had 'psychically' seen a girl and a short, petite woman with shoulder-length dark hair standing at the spot from where I had felt the breeze come. Try as I might, I had seen nothing.

After a break we continued the séance, and everyone was concentrating hard; I was lost completely in thought and near to forgetting where I was.

Until I was stunned by a sudden scream from right beside us.

A surge of fear and adrenaline coursed through me, and the rest of the group reacted with terrified yells or attempts to run away. I could feel the 'fight-or-flight' impulse, but I forced myself to stand where I was, firmly gripping the hands of the others so as not to break the séance circle. I had watched too many films to forget the importance of unity in the face of supernatural danger – or, as more likely, when attacked by a psychotic maniac. There was another strangled scream; this time it seemed to be further away, moving out of the woods.

It would have been truly amazing if not for David's revelation, told amid shaky laughter, that it had only been a pheasant – nothing ghostly or supernatural, just a bird that we had startled and which had shrieked as it flew away.

The WOLF team tries to follow a balanced approach, avoiding blind faith in the validity of any purported supernatural incident – but not discounting the *possibility* of real paranormal activity, not without rational analysis and investigation. "It's healthy to be a sceptic," said David, "but it's even better to keep an open mind."

"It can give people peace and calm"

Quite apart from trying to catch glimpse of unearthly spirits, WOLF has been at the forefront of the recent revolution in spiritual healing, offering their services and advice to the public.

Simone is enthusiastic in her support for the benefits of reiki (pronounced "ray-kee"), the Japanese art of hands-on healing which channels and uses the 'universal life-force' to facilitate self-healing energy and open up the body's chakras.

"It can give people peace and calm, revitalising the energy of the body," she said. "It doesn't claim to 'heal' physical problems, but it can sometimes help, it can get people enthused to heal, and in a frame of mind to do so."

Simone has been interested in spiritual growth and healing for some years, after the death of a close friend encouraging her to take a more active role in helping those in pain. She conducts workshops where she teaches reiki skills and techniques.

"We can't give it up!"

This hectic workload has had an impact on Simone and David, and it is not surprising that the past few years have also been draining for the rest of the WOLF team. Creating a new group for paranormal research and establishing its proud reputation can be inconvenienced by the necessity of a day-job.

"I'm so tired," said Simone, "asleep at 1am and up at 7am for work, sometimes going to bed later when we're on an overnight vigil. Sometimes I only get back at 4am, and it's hardly worth bothering with going to sleep."

They remain committed to the cause: "We have a passion for it," said David, "we've been pushed to our physical and emotional limits and we can't give it up!"

More information can be found

at the WOLF website

www.wolf-rs.co.uk

Contact the author

Ulysses525@yahoo.co.uk